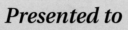

Presented to

_____

on

_____

With prayers and best wishes from

_____

_____

My Bible

The Story of God's Love

Written by Melissa Wright

Illustrated by Augusta Curreli

Pauline
BOOKS & MEDIA
Boston

Nihil Obstat: Reverend John L. Sullivan
Imprimatur: ✠ Archbishop Seán O'Malley, O.F.M.Cap.
January 13, 2004

Library of Congress Cataloging-in-Publication Data

Wright, Melissa.
 My Bible : the story of God's love / written by Melissa Wright ; illustrated by Augusta Curreli.
    p. cm.
 ISBN 0-8198-4834-4
 1. Bible stories, English. 2. Catholic Church—Doctrines—Juvenile lit-
erature. I. Curreli, Augusta. II. Title.

 BS551.3.W77 2004
 220.9'505—dc22

2004009051

English translation of the Doxology and The Apostles' Creed by the International Consultation on English Texts.

Published by Pauline Books & Media, 50 Saint Pauls Avenue, Boston, MA 02130-3491.

Printed in China

MBGL NAPCHIDONJN12-2100001 4834-4

www.pauline.org

Pauline Books & Media is the publishing house of the Daughters of St. Paul, an international congregation of women religious serving the Church with the communications media.

5 6 7 8 9 10 11   19 18 17 16 15

Contents

New Testament

God Speaks to Us

We have a wonderful Father in heaven who loves us and watches over us. Our wonderful Father is God. The more we know about God, the more we will love him. Because he is so great, we can never know all there is to know about him. If we learned about God every day of our lives, there would still be so much more to learn! God wants us to know who he is.

God speaks to us about himself in a special book called the Bible.

The Bible is God's way of letting us know his loving plan for us. This is the plan: God wants us to be with him forever! The Bible shows us that even when his people sometimes turned away from him, God did not forget his plan. He always found a way to call them back to him.

In the Bible, God tells us that he is the only God. Even before there was anything else, God was always there. He never had a beginning like we did.

In the one God, there are three Persons: the Father, the Son, and the Holy Spirit. The Father is God. The Son is God. The Holy Spirit is God. And yet, there is only one God. We cannot understand how this can be. God is much greater than our minds can understand!

God made us and loves us. *We are his people.* We want to give him glory. This means that we want to praise and honor God with all his people because he is so great.

Here is a prayer that tells how great God is:

Glory to the Father, and to the Son, and to the Holy Spirit, as it was in the beginning, is now, and will be forever. Amen.

Old Testament

God Made Everything

Genesis 1, 2

There was a time when there was no world. There were no sky and sun, no moon and stars. There were no trees or mountains or oceans. There were no animals and there were no people.

There was only God.

Then God began to make the world and everything that is in it.

God made everything out of nothing, just by wanting it to happen. Only God can do that! You can make things out of clay or paper. But only God can make things out of nothing at all. We call this "creating."

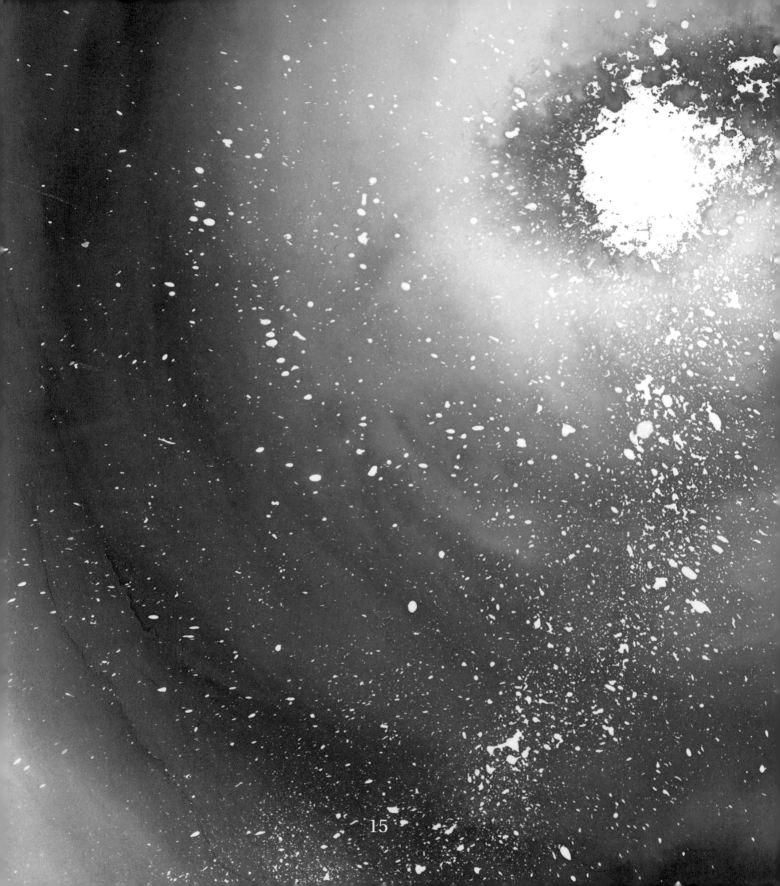

God made the sky above us with the sun and moon and stars.

He made the seas and lakes and rivers. He made all kinds of plants and trees. He made fish to swim in the water and birds to fly in the air. He made every kind of animal that lives on earth. God looked at the world and everything that he had made. He saw how beautiful it all was. Then God made the first man. He gave the man a soul that would live forever and a mind that could know who God was. God named the man Adam.

God wanted to put Adam in charge of all the animals that he had made. So God brought the animals to Adam to see what name he would give each one. Adam looked at them carefully. Adam named the camels and the dolphins. He named the field mice and the sparrows. He named every animal that lives on the earth, in the sea, or in the air. And when Adam was finished naming all God's creatures, he said, "None of the animals are like me."

Then, so Adam wouldn't be alone, God made the first woman. God brought the woman to Adam to be his partner. Adam named her Eve. They lived happily in the beautiful world God made.

The First Sin

Genesis 3

God gave Adam and Eve a lovely garden to live in. It was called Eden, which means "Garden of Delight." Adam and Eve were very happy in the Garden of Eden. It was full of beautiful fruit trees and colorful flowers. All the animals were gentle and peaceful.

Before creating the world, God had also created angels. The good angels live with God in heaven. God made them intelligent. He gave them the power to make their own choices. One of the angels chose to turn against God. He became a devil—an enemy of God. Other angels who decided to go along with the devil became devils, too.

The devil did not like to see Adam and Eve so happy. He wanted to make them disobey God as he had done. So he made himself look like a snake. The devil went into Eden and waited by the big tree in the middle of the garden. God had told Adam and Eve that they were not supposed to eat any fruit from this tree.

Before long, Eve walked by the tree. The snake asked her,

"Is it true that God won't let you eat the fruit from the trees in the garden?"

Eve answered, "No. We can eat from all the trees except this one."

"If you eat this fruit," the snake said, "you will become as wise as God." So Eve decided to listen to the snake instead of God. She took some fruit and tasted it. Then she brought some to Adam. He tasted it, too. Adam and Eve both disobeyed God. This was the first sin. That evening, Adam and Eve heard the sound of God walking in the garden. They hid from him because they knew they had done something wrong. But God sees us all the time. And he saw Adam and Eve. God loved Adam and Eve even though they had done something wrong, just as God loves us even when we do wrong things. God wants to help us do what is right.

Because of their sin, Adam and Eve could no longer live in the Garden of Eden. God gave them a place to live outside of the garden. Here they would have to work hard all day to grow their food. It was a sad life compared to life in Eden. Sin had changed everything.

Adam and Eve brought sin and sadness into God's beautiful world. But God still loved them and wanted them to be happy. God promised to save the world from sin. Adam and Eve weren't sure how God would do this. But we know that God's plan was to send his own Son to save us. God's Son, Jesus, would be our Savior. Jesus would have a very special mother named Mary. But the world would have to wait a long time for this to happen.

Cain and Abel

Genesis 4

Adam and Eve had two sons. They named them Cain and Abel. Abel became a shepherd, and Cain was a farmer.

After a while, Cain became jealous of Abel. God said to Cain, "Why are you angry? If you do what is right, you don't have to worry. Say 'no' to sin. You can if you want to!"

But Cain decided to kill his brother Abel. This was a terrible sin! God does

22

not want us to sin. He does not want us to hurt each other. After Cain killed Abel, God sent Cain away. Cain no longer had a home. He had to wander from place to place. But God still loved Cain and did not want anything bad to happen to him, so he promised to protect him.

Cain and Abel were born with the sin of their parents on their souls. It is called "original sin." We too are born with original sin, which comes to the whole human race from Adam and Eve.

When we are baptized, original sin is taken away from our soul. We become children of God. This means that Jesus is our brother and heaven is our homeland. Baptism makes us members of the Church. We have all these wonderful gifts from God because Jesus came to be our Savior, just as God promised Adam and Eve long ago.

Noah and the Great Flood

Genesis 6–9

Adam and Eve had other children too. When these children grew up, they had their own children, and there began to be more and more people on earth. As time went by, most people began to disobey God. When God saw how evil they had become, he was sorry that he had made them.

But there was a very good man named Noah. Noah and his family loved and obeyed God. God told Noah that he was going to take away almost all the living things on earth because of people's sinfulness. But God would keep Noah and his family safe so they could start a new family of people who would listen to the Lord.

God told Noah to build an ark out of wood. (The ark was a kind of big boat.) Noah and his family obeyed. "Go into the ark with your family, Noah," God said. "Bring with you two of every kind of animal. This way you and the animals will be safe when I send a

25

flood to wash away all the wickedness from the earth."

Noah brought his family into the ark. He brought all the animals into the ark, two by two. He stored up enough food for his family and all the animals.

In one week it started to rain. For forty days and forty nights it rained and rained. The water got deeper and deeper and lifted the ark up off the ground. The water covered even the highest mountains! Every living thing on earth was wiped out by the flood—everyone and everything except Noah and his family and the animals they had with them. They were all safe and sound in the ark.

Finally the rain stopped. The deep water started to go down. The ark was now on the top of Mount Ararat. Noah couldn't see how high the water was, so he opened a little window in the ark and sent out a big black bird and a dove. The water was still so high that the birds couldn't find a place to rest. They flew back to the ark.

A week later Noah sent the dove out again. The dove flew until it came to an olive tree. It broke off one of the branches with its beak and came back to the ark. Now Noah knew that the water was below the tops of the trees! After another week, Noah sent out the dove again. This time the dove did not come back to the ark. It had found a home and food. Noah knew it was time to leave the ark. So he and his family and all the animals went out into the sunshine. The world sparkled like new! Noah watched as all the birds from the ark soared into the air. Then he saw a beautiful rainbow stretching from one end of the sky to the other.

"The rainbow is a sign of my promise to love and watch over all living things," God told Noah. Noah and his family were so happy. They would be the new beginning of human life on earth, and they knew that God would love and protect them.

God Calls Abram

Genesis 12, 13

A long time after the great flood there lived a man named Abram. Abram had a beautiful wife named Sarai. One day God told Abram, "I want you to leave this place and go to a new land that I will show you. I will make you and your family a great nation. I will bless you, Abram, and make you a blessing for many people."

So Abram packed up all his things. He took his wife Sarai and his nephew Lot and did as the Lord told him. He brought his family to the land of Canaan. When they got there, God said, "I will give this land to you and your family, Abram."

After that, Abram and his family went down to Egypt, where they became very rich. Then they returned to the land in Canaan that God had promised to Abram. But Abram and Lot had a problem. There was not enough land for all their sheep and cattle.

Abram said to Lot, "We should split up. Choose the land to the left or to the right. I will take what's left." Lot chose the better land to the east and went to live there.

After Lot left, the Lord said to Abram, "Look all around you as far as you can see. I will give all this land to you and your family forever." Abram put his faith in God and worshiped him.

Abraham and Sarah

Genesis 15, 17, 18

Abram and Sarai were very old, and they had no children. But God told Abram that he would have a big family that would become a great nation. Abram asked God, "How can this happen when I have no children?"

"I am God the Almighty," God answered. "Walk with me and do what is right and I will make you the father of many nations." Abraham put his trust in God and believed all that God told him. Then God changed Abram's name to Abraham because of this promise they made to each other. God also changed Sarai's name to Sarah and promised that she would have a baby boy. Abraham and Sarah laughed at this because they had never heard of elderly people having a baby. Abraham was already one hundred, and Sarah was ninety! But God said, "Is anything too much for the Lord to do? At this time next year, you will have a son."

And that is just what happened! Abraham and Sarah named their baby boy Isaac, which means "laughter," since they both laughed when God told them they would have a son. Little Isaac brought joy and laughter to his parents in their old age.

Because Abraham believed what God said, we call him "our father in faith." We have faith when we believe all that God has told us through the Bible and through the Church. God can never make a mistake or tell us something that is not true. He deserves all our trust.

Jacob and Esau

Genesis 23–25

After his wife died, Abraham sent a servant to his home-land to choose a wife for his son Isaac, who was now grown up. The servant came back with a beautiful woman named Rebekah, and she and Isaac were married.

After a long life, Abraham died. He was buried next to his wife Sarah.

For many years Isaac and Rebekah had no children. Finally, they had twin boys. They named the twins Esau and Jacob. Esau was born first. Then came

Jacob. The two boys were very different. As they got older, Esau became a skillful hunter. But Jacob liked to stay at home. Esau was his father's favorite son, and Jacob was his mother's favorite son.

One day Jacob was at home cooking a stew. Esau came in and said, "Let me have that stew! I'm starving!" Jacob said, "I'll trade it for your birthright." (Since Esau had been born first, he had the right to a special place of honor in the family. He would also inherit twice as much of his father's possessions.) Jacob wanted Esau to sell him these special privileges. All Esau could think of was how hungry he was, so he agreed and sold Jacob his rights as the first-born son. Esau gulped down the stew without thinking about what he had done.

Jacob's Trick

Genesis 27

When Isaac was very old and couldn't see very well, he called his older son Esau and said, "I am near the end of my life. Go hunt some meat for me. Prepare a nice meal with whatever you catch. After I eat it, I will give you my special blessing before I die."

Rebekah was listening to what Isaac told Esau. She thought of a way that Jacob could trick Isaac into giving him the blessing instead.

(This was not right, but Jacob agreed to the plan.) As soon as Esau left to go hunting, Rebekah sent Jacob out to get two young goats from the ock. Rebekah used the goat meat to cook a meal that she knew her husband Isaac would like.

Now Jacob had very smooth skin but Esau had hairy skin. So Rebekah covered Jacob's hands and neck with pieces of goatskin. "If your father touches you," she explained to Jacob, "he will think you are Esau." Rebekah also gave Jacob some of Esau's best clothes to wear. Then she handed him the meal she had prepared.

Jacob brought the dish to Isaac. "Which one of my sons are you?" asked Isaac.

"I am Esau, your first-born son," Jacob answered. "Here is the meal I prepared. Eat it, and then give me your blessing."

"How did you do get this meal ready so quickly?" Isaac asked.

"The Lord helped me," Jacob answered.

Isaac couldn't see well, but he knew the voice didn't sound like Esau's. He touched Jacob's hands and neck. They felt hairy because of the goatskins. Isaac also smelled the fragrance of Esau's borrowed clothes. So Isaac believed it was Esau. He ate the meal. Then Isaac gave Jacob this blessing:

"May God give you plenty of grain and wine. Let people from other lands serve you and give you honor. Whoever blesses you will be blessed."

As soon as Jacob left, Esau came in with the meal he had prepared from his hunt. "Here is the meat I brought you, Father," Esau said. "Eat it and give me your blessing."

"Who are you?" Isaac asked.

"I am Esau, your first-born!"

When Isaac heard this he began to shake. "Someone was here before you and gave me a meal to eat. I gave *him* the blessing!"

Esau cried out, "Bless me too, Father!"

"Your brother Jacob tricked me into giving him the blessing that was meant for you," Isaac said, shaking his head. "I could only give that blessing once."

But because Esau kept begging his father for a blessing too, Isaac finally gave him a different kind of blessing.

Jacob's Adventures

Genesis 27–33

Esau was angry with Jacob because Jacob had tricked their father into giving him the special blessing. Esau even wanted to kill Jacob. Their mother Rebekah was very worried. She decided to send Jacob to live with her brother Laban. Jacob had to walk to his

40

Uncle Laban's home. It was over 500 miles away!

That first night, Jacob stopped to sleep. He used a stone for a pillow. Soon Jacob began to dream. In his dream he saw a stairway going all the way up to heaven. Angels were going up and down on it. Jacob heard the Lord tell him, "I am the God of your fathers Abraham and Isaac. I will give this land to you and to your children after you. Your future family will be as countless as the dust of the earth.

They will be a blessing for all the nations. Wherever you go, I will keep you safe and bring you back to this land."

Jacob woke up and cried out, "The Lord is really here, even though I didn't know it! This place is the gateway to heaven!" Then Jacob made this promise: "If God helps me on my journey, and gives me food, clothing, and his protection, so that one day I get back to my father's house safely, then the Lord shall be my God. This stone that I slept on shall be the house of God, and I will give back to the Lord one tenth of all he gives to me."

And God did watch over Jacob. Jacob finally reached his Uncle Laban's house. There he fell in love with Laban's beautiful daughter Rachel.

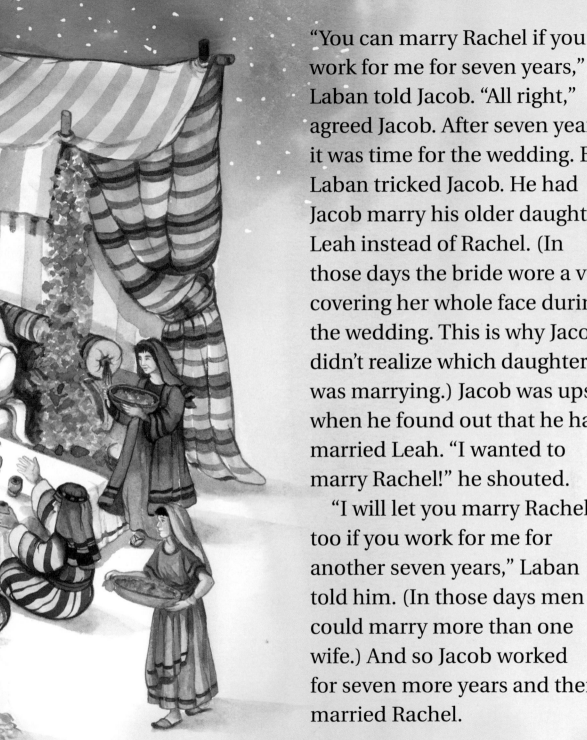

"You can marry Rachel if you work for me for seven years," Laban told Jacob. "All right," agreed Jacob. After seven years it was time for the wedding. But Laban tricked Jacob. He had Jacob marry his older daughter Leah instead of Rachel. (In those days the bride wore a veil covering her whole face during the wedding. This is why Jacob didn't realize which daughter he was marrying.) Jacob was upset when he found out that he had married Leah. "I wanted to marry Rachel!" he shouted.

"I will let you marry Rachel too if you work for me for another seven years," Laban told him. (In those days men could marry more than one wife.) And so Jacob worked for seven more years and then married Rachel.

Later on, Jacob decided to go back to Canaan, his homeland. He took his wives and twelve children, his servants, and all his flocks and began the journey. Jacob knew that his brother Esau was living in Edom. Jacob and his family would have to pass through Edom to get to Canaan. Jacob was hoping that Esau had forgiven him for having tricked his father. He sent some messengers ahead to meet Esau. The messengers came back and reported, "Esau is coming to meet you with 400 men, Jacob."

Now Jacob was afraid. He thought that Esau and his men were coming to fight. He prayed, "O God, you told me you would take care of me. I don't deserve your kindness,

but please save me from my brother Esau!"

Then Jacob chose some of his goats, sheep, camels, cattle and donkeys. He sent them ahead of him as a gift to Esau. Jacob hoped that when Esau received this gift he would forgive him.

At last Jacob saw Esau coming toward him with the 400 men. Jacob walked ahead of his family and bowed to the ground. All of a sudden Esau ran toward Jacob. He threw his arms around him and kissed him. Now Jacob knew that Esau had forgiven him! After this happy meeting Esau went back to Edom and Jacob and his family continued on their journey to Canaan.

Joseph and His Brothers

Genesis 37

Jacob finally arrived in Canaan. But his wife Rachel had died on the way there. Her sons, Joseph and Benjamin, became Jacob's favorites. Since Jacob loved Joseph more than his other sons, he gave him a nice new robe. It had many different colors and was very beautiful. This made Jacob's other sons begin to hate Joseph. When they saw him coming, they wouldn't even say hello.

One night Joseph had a dream. Later, he told his brothers all about it: "We were tying bundles of grain in the fields. All of a sudden, my bundle of grain stood up straight, and all your bundles bowed down to it."

Joseph's brothers thought the dream meant that Joseph would make himself a king over them. This made them hate him even more.

Soon after this, Joseph told his brothers about another dream he had had. "The sun, the moon, and eleven stars were bowing down to me." Joseph told the dream to his father Jacob too. Jacob wasn't happy about it. He said, "Do you mean to tell me that your mother and I and your brothers are supposed to bow down to you?"

Joseph made his brothers angry and jealous with all his bragging. When they saw that Joseph was also their father's favorite son, it made things even worse. The brothers got so jealous and so angry that they finally did something terrible....

One day, Joseph's brothers had taken their flocks to a pasture far away. Jacob sent Joseph to see how they were doing. When they saw him coming, his brothers decided to kill him and throw him into a dry well. "We can tell Father that a wild animal ate Joseph," one of the brothers said. "Yes!" the others agreed.

But Reuben, the oldest of the brothers, didn't want to kill Joseph. "Let's just throw him into the well," he said. (Reuben's plan was to pull Joseph out later and

bring him back to his father.) So when Joseph came up to them, his brothers grabbed him, tore off his colorful robe, and threw him into the dry well.

Just then, some traders came by. They were on their way to Egypt. Judah, one of the brothers, had an idea: "Why don't we sell Joseph to these traders? After all, he is our brother, and we shouldn't kill him." So they sold Joseph as a slave for twenty pieces of silver. Then they killed one of their goats and dipped Joseph's robe into the blood. Next the brothers sent a messenger to bring the robe to their father Jacob. When Jacob saw it he cried out, "A wild animal has torn Joseph to pieces!" Jacob was very sad and wept for his son for many days.

Joseph the Slave

Genesis 39, 40

The traders took Joseph to Egypt. They sold him as a slave to a man named Potiphar. Potiphar was an officer of Pharaoh, the king of Egypt. The Lord was with Joseph, and things went well for him. Potiphar was so pleased with Joseph's work that he put him in charge of his whole household.

After a while, Potiphar's wife tried to get Joseph to do something wrong. But Joseph didn't want to displease his master Potiphar. He also didn't want to offend God. "I will not do what you want," Joseph told Potiphar's wife. "It's not right." This made Potiphar's wife very angry. She lied to Potiphar and said that Joseph had done something wrong when he really hadn't. Potiphar believed his wife and threw Joseph into the royal prison.

But God was with Joseph even in jail. The chief jailer trusted Joseph. "I'm putting you in charge of all the other prisoners," he told him.

A little while later, Pharaoh put the royal cupbearer and

51

baker in jail. On the same night they each had a dream. The next morning, Joseph noticed that they were very upset. "We're upset because of the dreams we had," they told Joseph. "Tell me about them," Joseph said. They did, and Joseph explained what the dreams meant.

Two years later, Pharaoh had two strange dreams. In one, he was standing by the Nile River when seven fat cows came up out of the river to graze on the bank. Right behind them, seven skinny cows came out of the river and ate the seven fat cows. Then Pharaoh woke up.

When he went back to sleep, he had another dream. This time he saw seven healthy ears of grain growing on one stalk. Right behind them grew seven thin and sickly ears of grain. The

seven thin ears swallowed the seven healthy ears. Then Pharaoh woke up again.

In the morning, Pharaoh was disturbed because none of his wise men could explain the dreams to him. Then the royal cupbearer told Pharaoh how Joseph had explained his dream when he was in jail. So Pharaoh had Joseph brought to him from jail. He described his dreams to Joseph. "Tell me what they mean," Pharaoh said, "because I've heard you are good at explaining dreams."

Joseph answered, "It is God who will help me explain the dreams to you. The seven fat cows and the seven healthy ears of grain stand for seven years when there will be more than enough food in Egypt. After that, there will be a food shortage for seven years. The seven skinny cows and the seven sickly ears of grain stand for the food shortage."

Then Joseph gave Pharaoh a suggestion. "You should find a wise man and put him in charge of the land. During the seven years of plenty, the extra food should be stored away and kept for the seven years when the land will not grow any food.

This way, the people will have enough to eat during the food shortage."

Pharaoh was very happy with Joseph's explanation and plan. "I pick you to be the one in charge of Egypt's fields!" he exclaimed. Pharaoh dressed Joseph in fine clothes and gave him a gold chain to wear around his neck. Except for Pharaoh himself, Joseph was the most important man in all of Egypt!

Joseph's Brothers Come to Egypt

Genesis 41–43

Now that Joseph was serving Pharaoh, he traveled all through Egypt. He made sure that during the seven years of plenty the extra food was stored in all the towns. There was so much grain stored that he couldn't measure it anymore!

After the seven years of plenty ended, the seven years of shortage began. The land stopped growing grain, and people in all the countries of the world ran out of food. But Pharaoh told the Egyptians to go to Joseph for help. So Joseph opened up the storehouses of grain and made sure that everyone got their share. People from other countries found out that there was grain in Egypt, and they came from all over to buy it from Joseph.

Back in Canaan, Jacob and his family had run out of food. So Jacob sent his sons to Egypt to buy grain. But he kept his youngest son, Benjamin, home with him. He was afraid something would happen to him.

When the brothers appeared before Joseph in Egypt, he recognized them right away. But because he was shaved and wearing fine Egyptian clothes, they didn't know he was their brother Joseph. They bowed down before him, just as Joseph had dreamed long ago that they would. But Joseph spoke harshly to them and called them spies. The brothers tried to explain themselves. They told Joseph about their father Jacob and their youngest brother who was at home with him. "We had another brother named Joseph," they explained, "but he is gone now."

Joseph listened to everything. Then he said, "I will give you a test. One of you will be kept here in prison. The rest of you can take your share of grain home to your families. But you must bring back your youngest brother so I can see if you are being honest or not."

The brothers exclaimed to one another, "Now we are being punished for what we did to our brother Joseph!" When Joseph heard this, he turned away and wept. Then Simeon was put in prison while the rest of the brothers were allowed to go back to their father Jacob in Canaan.

When the nine brothers returned home, they told their father all that had happened. But Jacob did not want to lose Benjamin as he had lost Joseph, and now Simeon. He would not let his sons go back to Egypt.

Then the food shortage got even worse, and Jacob and his family used up all their grain. Jacob had no choice but to send his sons, including Benjamin, back to Egypt.

At their arrival, they were surprised to be invited to dinner in Joseph's house. When Joseph came in, the brothers bowed down before him. "How are you, and how is your father?" Joseph asked. Then Joseph noticed his youngest brother Benjamin. The love he felt for Benjamin was so strong that Joseph had to leave the room so that his brothers wouldn't see him cry. Later he went back in and ordered the meal to be served.

59

The Reunion

Genesis 44–46

It was time for Joseph's brothers to go back to Canaan. (They still did not realize that Joseph was their brother.) Joseph gave them all the food they could carry back in their bags. He also hid his silver cup in Benjamin's bag.

Once they were out of the city, Joseph sent a servant after the brothers. The servant searched their bags for the missing silver cup. When the cup was found in Benjamin's bag, the brothers were brought back to Joseph's house.

The brothers were afraid. They threw themselves on the ground in front of Joseph.

Judah spoke for all of them: "What can we say? How can we prove our innocence? We are your slaves!"

But Joseph replied, "Only the one who stole my silver cup

61

will be my slave. The rest of you may go home."

Judah went up to Joseph and pleaded with him. "If we go back home without Benjamin, our father will die of sorrow. I promised to bring him home safe and sound. Please let him go with the others and keep me here as your slave in his place."

Joseph couldn't hide his feelings any longer. He ordered everyone else to leave so that he and his brothers were alone in the room. He began to weep loudly and said, "I am Joseph, your brother! You sold me as a slave and I ended up in Egypt. But don't be upset or blame yourselves. God was working out a plan to save lives by sending me here ahead of you."

His brothers were so surprised they couldn't even speak!

Joseph continued, "Go home quickly and bring back our father! Tell him I am alive and that God has made me master of all of Egypt! Bring our whole family to Egypt—children, grandchildren, flocks, herds, everything you have! I will make sure you have all you need while the food shortage lasts." Then Joseph threw his arms around Benjamin and they both wept for joy. He kissed all his brothers and finally they were able to speak again.

The brothers went back to Canaan with wagons and supplies. They joyfully told their father, "Joseph is alive! He is the ruler of Egypt! He wants us all to go to Egypt to live there!"

So Jacob and his children and grandchildren took all they owned and moved to Egypt. They settled in the land of Goshen. They lived there many years and the family grew and grew.

Moses Is Born

Exodus 1, 2

Jacob's family, the Israelites, continued to grow in Egypt, even after Joseph and his brothers had died. Egypt's new Pharaoh didn't know about Joseph. He was upset because there were so many Israelites in Egypt. He was afraid that if there were a war, the Israelites would take the side of Egypt's enemies. So Pharaoh forced the Israelites to be slaves. They had to do the hard work of building cities and working in the fields. But the Israelites kept on growing in number. When Pharaoh saw this, he gave this order: "All the Israelite baby boys are to be thrown into the Nile River and drowned."

A family from the line of Joseph's brother Levi had a baby boy. His mother kept him hidden at home as long as she could. When he was three months old, she put him in a basket woven from reeds and placed it on the riverbank. The baby's sister hid nearby to watch her brother and to see what would happen.

Soon the daughter of Pharaoh came down to the river with her maids. She noticed the basket and had it brought to her. When she opened the basket and found the baby inside crying,

Pharaoh's daughter felt sorry for him. She knew he was one of the Israelite babies. She knew that his mother was hiding him to save his life.

The baby's sister came forward and asked, "Would you like me to get one of the Israelite women to nurse the baby for you?"

Pharaoh's daughter answered, "Yes, please do."

So the girl ran home and brought her own mother to the riverbank where Pharaoh's daughter was waiting. The mother brought her son back home and nursed him. When he was a little older, she took him to Pharaoh's daughter, who adopted him. Pharaoh's daughter gave the little boy the name Moses. She brought him up as her own son in the royal palace of Pharaoh.

The Burning Bush

Exodus 2–4

When Moses was grown up, he went to visit the Israelite slaves to see what their life was like. He saw an Egyptian beating an Israelite, and he became very angry. Since no one was around, Moses killed the Egyptian and buried him in the sand. The next day, he found out that other people knew what he had done. Even Pharaoh had heard about it and was upset. So Moses ran away to the land of Midian.

In Midian, Moses met a man named Jethro, who had seven daughters. "Stay here and live with us, Moses," Jethro invited. So Moses did. Moses married Zipporah, Jethro's oldest daughter. He became a shepherd and took care of Jethro's flock.

One day, Moses led the flock of sheep to a mountain called Horeb. There he saw a bush that was on fire but did not get burned up. When he went over for a closer look, he heard the voice of God calling to him from the bush, "Moses! Moses!"

"Here I am!" Moses answered.

God said, "Don't come any closer! Take off your sandals because you are on holy ground. I am the God of Abraham, Isaac, and Jacob. I have seen the suffering of my people. I will rescue them from Egypt and bring them into a wide-open land flowing with milk and honey. I am sending you to Pharaoh to lead my people out of Egypt."

Moses said to God, "How can I go to Pharaoh and lead the Israelites out of Egypt?"

"I will be with you," God promised. "And after you lead my people out of Egypt, you will worship me on this mountain."

"But what if the Israelites ask me what your name is?" Moses asked.

"I am the One who is," God told him. "Tell the Israelites, 'I AM sent me to you.' Gather the leaders of Israel and tell them that I am concerned about how my people are being treated. Then go with the leaders to Pharaoh. Ask him to let the Israelites travel to the desert to offer sacrifice to me. I know the king won't let you leave, so I will work wonders to show my power. Then he will let you go." And God gave Moses a walking stick with which he would perform miracles.

Moses left for Egypt, taking the walking stick with him. God sent Aaron, the brother of Moses, to meet him in the desert. Moses told Aaron all that God was going to do, and together they went to the leaders of Israel. Aaron was a better speaker, so he spoke for Moses. He told the Israelite leaders everything that God had said. And Moses performed miracles to prove that God was with them.

The Israelites believed Moses and Aaron, and they worshiped God who cared so much about them in their sufferings.

The Ten Plagues

Exodus 5–11

Moses and Aaron went to Pharaoh and said, "The Lord God of Israel says to let the people go into the desert."

But Pharaoh's answer was, "Why should I listen to the God of Israel?" He would not let the Israelites go, and he made them work even harder.

Then the people complained to Moses and Aaron, "It's your fault things are worse for us than before."

So Moses prayed to the Lord God, and God said, "Now you will see my mighty deeds. I will free my people from slavery and bring them to the land I promised to Abraham, Isaac, and Jacob."

God sent Moses and Aaron back to Pharaoh. Aaron threw his walking stick to the ground and it turned into a snake! Then Pharaoh's magicians threw their walking staffs down, and they were turned into snakes too. But Moses' staff swallowed the magicians' staffs! Even after this, Pharaoh was stubborn and would not listen to Moses and Aaron.

So God showed Pharaoh his power by sending ten plagues, or punishments, on the Egyptians.

When Aaron struck the waters of the Nile River with his walking staff, and then held the staff out toward the land around him, all the water in Egypt was turned to blood. This was the first plague.

After this, God sent more plagues through Moses, one after another. Thousands of frogs came out of the river and filled the land and homes of the Egyptians. Then there were swarms of little insects everywhere.

After that there was a sickness that killed the horses, herds, and flocks of the Egyptians.

But the Israelites' animals stayed healthy.

Next, the people and animals of Egypt had blisters and sores on their skin, but not the Israelites.

Then a terrible hailstorm destroyed all the crops. When the hailstorm was over, God sent locusts, like grasshoppers, that ate whatever was left of the ruined crops.

The ninth plague was a darkness so deep that it could be felt. For three days the Egyptians could not even move because of the darkness.

But even after all these terrible signs, Pharaoh was stubborn and wouldn't let the Israelites go. God told Moses that after the tenth and last plague, Pharaoh would beg them to leave.

Moses gave Pharaoh the Lord's message: "Tonight at midnight, I the Lord will pass through Egypt and take the life of every first-born child, from the first-born of Pharaoh to the first-born of the servants, even the first-born of the animals." But Pharaoh still would not listen to Moses.

God is the Lord of life. All life comes from God who created us out of love. Only God has the right to give life or to take it away.

The First Passover

Exodus 12

God gave Moses special instructions for the Israelites on the night on which the last plague took place. Each Israelite family was to take a lamb and kill it at twilight, the time right after sunset. Each family was also supposed to

mark the door of their house with some of the lamb's blood. Then they roasted the lamb and ate it with flat, hard bread and bitter herbs. They ate with their sandals on and their walking sticks in their hands. They were ready to leave Egypt in a hurry.

On that same night, God went through the land taking the life of every first-born in Egypt. But when the Lord saw the lambs' blood marking the doors of the Israelites' houses, he passed over them, leaving their first-born unharmed. That is why this special night was called "Passover."

In all the Egyptian homes, the life of each first-born was taken, from the first-born of Pharaoh to the first-born of the prisoners in jail. Even the first-born of the animals died. At midnight, the Egyptians woke up and began to cry loudly. Someone had died in every one of their houses.

Pharaoh called for Moses right away. "Take your people and go away from here!" he exclaimed. "Take your flocks and herds and leave!"

So the Israelites left Egypt in a hurry.

God led his people through the desert toward the Red Sea. He went before them as a pillar of cloud during the day and as a pillar of fire during the night. This way, they could see their way both day and night, and they knew that the Lord was with them.

Some time after the Israelites had left Egypt, Pharaoh suddenly changed his mind and sent his army to get them and bring them back. The soldiers caught up with Moses and the Israelites by the Red Sea.

The Israelites cried out in fear when they saw the Egyptian

soldiers. But Moses shouted, "Don't be afraid! God is with us, fighting for us. This will be the last we see of the Egyptians!"

Then God told Moses, "Tell the people to move ahead. Lift your staff out over the sea and split it in two. Then you will all be able to go across on dry land." Moses did as God commanded. The water separated, and the people walked through the middle of the sea with a wall of water on their left and on their right.

The Egyptian army followed close behind. But once the Israelites were safely on the other side, God told Moses to raise his hand over the sea. The water suddenly flowed back into place and covered the Egyptians!

When the Israelites saw how God had saved them from the power of the Egyptians, they sang a song of praise and thanksgiving: "I will sing to the Lord, for he is gloriously triumphant."

The Ten Commandments

Exodus 16–20

Moses led the Israelites from the Red Sea through the desert. After a while the people started to complain because they were hungry and thirsty. But God was taking care of them. Each day the morning dew brought manna, a flaky kind of bread. And sometimes God also sent birds called quail for them to eat. For water, God told Moses to strike a rock with his walking staff in front of all the people. When Moses did this, water flowed out from the rock! God provided for the Israelites the whole time they were in the desert.

After three months, the Israelites came to a big mountain called Sinai. Here,

God promised that if the Israelites would obey him, they would be his special people. The people promised to do everything God asked.

Then God called Moses to the top of the mountain. He wanted to give the people his holy laws, so that they would know how he wanted them to live. These laws would make the Israelites different from all other people on earth. By obeying them, they would be God's holy people.

These are the laws or ten commandments that God gave Moses on Mount Sinai:

1. I am the Lord your God who saved you from slavery in Egypt. You must put me first, because no one is greater than I.

2. You must use my name with love and respect, because it is holy.

3. You must keep the Lord's day holy. It is a day of prayer and rest from work.

4. Obey your parents. Love and respect them so that you will live a long life in the land I am giving you.

5. You must not kill or hurt anyone. I want my people to be kind to one another.

6. You must keep yourselves pure. Married people must keep their promises to each other.

7. You must be honest and not take what belongs to someone else.

8. You must not tell lies.

9. You must be pure in your thoughts.

10. You must not even want to take anything that belongs to your neighbor.

When Moses told the people the laws that God had given them, they all cried out, "We will do everything God says!"

Ruth

Ruth 1–4

After Moses died, God chose Joshua to lead the Israelites into Canaan, the land he had promised to give them. The people settled the land and became farmers.

Once, during a food shortage, a family moved from Bethlehem to a land called Moab. While they were there, the father died and his widow, Naomi, was left with her two sons. The sons married Moabite women. After ten years, Naomi's sons died too, so she decided to go back to Bethlehem.

Naomi said to her two daughters-in-law, "You were kind to me and my sons; may the Lord be kind to you. Go back to your own mothers. The Lord will give you each a husband and a nice home." Sadly, she kissed them good-bye.

But one of them, Ruth, decided to stay with Naomi. She said to her mother-in-law, "I will go with you and live with you, wherever that may be. Your people will be my people, and your God will be my God. I will remain with you all my life and be buried where you are buried." So Naomi let Ruth return with her to Bethlehem.

At harvest time, Ruth went to a nearby field to pick up the grain that the workers left behind. The field belonged to a man named Boaz, who was an important relative of Naomi's.

When Boaz saw Ruth, he said to her, "Do not gather grain in any other field. You may stay with my women servants. No one will bother you. And when you need a drink, get some water from my workers."

Ruth bowed low and said, "Why are you so kind to me?"

Boaz replied, "I have heard all about your kindness to Naomi, how you left your own family and country to come to a strange new place. May the God of Israel reward you!"

Naomi was very happy when she found out about the kindness of Boaz toward

Ruth. It seemed to her that the two should be married. Boaz agreed.

Ruth and Boaz did get married. After a while they had a baby boy named Obed. Naomi helped to take care of him. She was comforted to have a grandson after having lost her husband and two sons.

When Obed grew up, he became the father of Jesse. And Jesse became the father of King David.

Hannah and Samuel

1 Samuel 1–3

A woman named Hannah was very sad because she had no children. She went with her husband to visit the shrine of the Lord at Shiloh. While she was there, Hannah went to the Temple to pray for a child. She promised that if she had a son, she would dedicate him to the Lord. Eli, the priest of the Temple, heard Hannah praying. He told her, "Go in peace, and may the Lord answer your prayer."

Soon after, Hannah had a baby boy and named him Samuel. She remembered her promise. When Samuel was old enough, Hannah brought him to the Temple at Shiloh. Hannah left Samuel with Eli the priest, who would be his teacher. Whenever Hannah visited Samuel, she brought him something to wear that she had made herself. To reward Hannah for offering Samuel to his service, the Lord gave her three more sons and two daughters.

Once while Samuel was asleep in the Temple, he heard someone call him. He thought it was Eli, so he ran to where Eli was sleeping and said, "Here I am. I heard you call." But Eli said, "I didn't call you. Go back to sleep." This happened three times. Then Eli realized the Lord was calling the boy. So he told Samuel, "When you are called again, say, 'Speak, Lord. I am listening.'"

Samuel went back to sleep until the Lord called him again.

This time he answered, "Speak, Lord. I am listening."

The Lord was with Samuel as he grew, and everyone realized that he was a prophet, chosen by God to speak to the people.

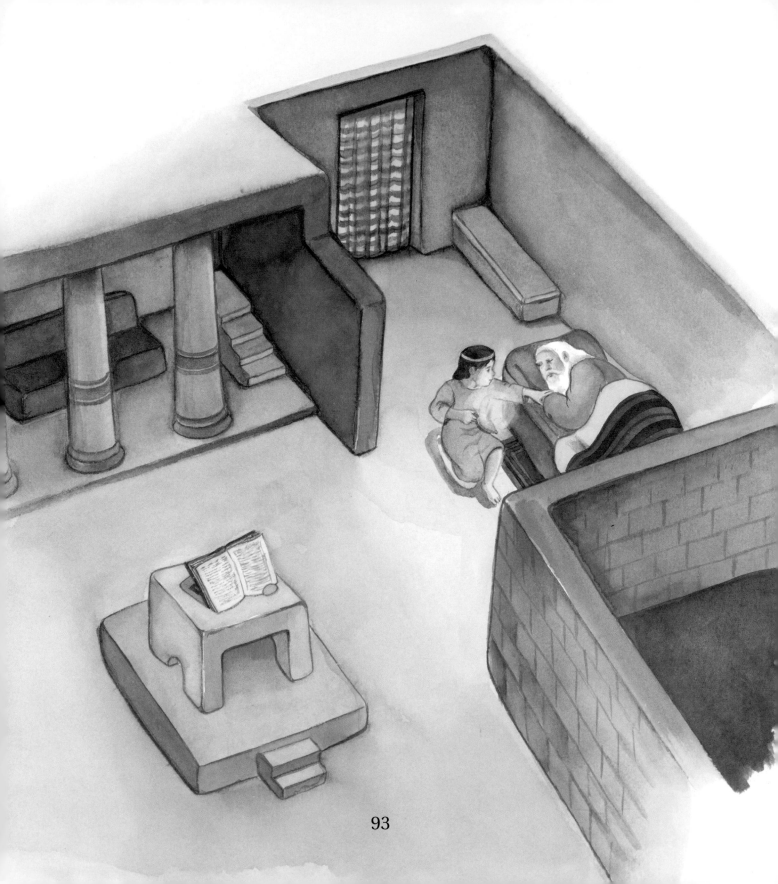

Saul Becomes King

1 Samuel 8–13

When Samuel was old, he let his sons be judges of Israel in his place. But they did not judge fairly as he had, so the leaders of Israel asked Samuel to give them a king instead. This way they could be like the other nations, which also had kings.

94

Samuel prayed to the Lord. "Listen to the people," God told him. God also told Samuel that he would send to him a man from the tribe of Benjamin. "This man will be the new king of Israel," God said.

Later, Samuel saw a man named Saul coming to meet him. The Lord told Samuel, "This is the one who will rule my people." So Samuel invited Saul to eat with him as his guest of honor. The next day, Samuel poured oil on Saul's head as a sign that God had chosen him to be king. After that, Samuel called all the Israelites together and showed them their new king. The people all shouted, "Long live the king!"

The Israelites had many enemies, especially the Philistines. King Saul bravely led his army and won many battles. But Saul was disobedient and twice he did the opposite of what God had commanded. So God told Samuel that he would find another king to take Saul's place.

David and Goliath

1 Samuel 16–17

God sent Samuel to Bethlehem to a man named Jesse. One of Jesse's sons would take Saul's place as king.

Samuel saw Jesse's son Eliab. He was handsome and tall. Samuel thought, *This must be the new king.* But God told Samuel, "I have not chosen him. You judge a person by his looks, but I see into the heart."

One by one, seven of Jesse's sons were introduced to Samuel. But each time, Samuel said, "The Lord has not chosen this one." Then he found out that the youngest son, David, was out watching the sheep. Samuel sent for David. When he came in, the Lord told Samuel, "This is the one!" So Samuel poured oil on David's head to show that he was the one that God had chosen.

Meanwhile, King Saul was sad and upset because the Lord's spirit had left him. He asked his servants to find someone who could play the harp to calm him. One of his servants told him about David, who played the harp and was also a good soldier. So Saul sent for David.

97

At that time Israel was at war against the Philistines. One of the Philistine soldiers, Goliath, came forward and shouted, "Choose one of your men to fight me! If he kills me, we will be your slaves. But if I kill him, then you must be our slaves!" And he insulted the army of Israel. Saul and his army were terrified, because Goliath was about eight or nine feet tall! He wore a bronze helmet and armor and held a huge sword in his hand. No one wanted to fight him!

But David begged Saul, "Let me fight that Philistine!"

Saul said, "No. You're too young!"

David replied, "If I could kill lions and bears when I was watching my sheep, I can surely kill this Philistine who is insulting the Lord's army!"

So Saul answered, "Go on, then! The Lord is with you!"

When Goliath saw David, who was just a boy, coming out to meet him, he laughed at him and called him names. David shouted back, "You fight with your sword and spear, but I fight in the name of the God of Israel!"

The two moved toward each other. David quickly loaded his slingshot and shot a stone at Goliath. The stone hit him in the forehead and he fell to the ground. David ran to take Goliath's sword and cut off his head. The rest of the Philistine army turned and ran away in fear.

After this, David was put in charge of Saul's army. Everyone was shouting praises for David, singing songs about what a great soldier he was! And Saul became angry and jealous when he realized that everyone liked David better.

David Becomes King

1 Samuel 18–31; 2 Samuel

The more successful David was, the more King Saul grew angry and jealous. David had to stay in hiding for a long time because Saul was always looking for him to kill him.

Twice, David had the chance to kill Saul, but he wouldn't do it. He respected Saul as the king, chosen by God. Even though Saul knew that David had spared his life, Saul still wanted to kill him.

The Philistines once again came to fight against Israel. When Saul saw their army, he was afraid. Samuel, who

100

had died, appeared to Saul in a vision. "Because you have disobeyed God, you will die in battle tomorrow," Samuel told Saul. And that is just what happened.

When David heard that Saul and his sons had died in battle, he was very sad. He sang a song in memory of Saul, praising his bravery.

Then David became the king of Israel. His army won many battles against their enemies, especially the Philistines. David tried to be a good king and do what God wanted. Once, he committed a serious sin, but he was sorry for it afterward, and God forgave him.

At the end of David's life, he told his son Solomon, "Be brave and obey the Lord. He will be with you to help you now that you are the king of Israel."

When David died, he was buried in the City of David. Solomon, David's son, became the new king. King Solomon obeyed God's commands. God gave him the gift of wisdom so that he could be a good ruler.

The Prophet Elijah

1 Kings 16–18

Not all of Israel's kings followed the Lord as King David had done. King Ahab did many evil things. He even built a temple to Baal, a false god, and worshiped him.

Elijah was a prophet who spoke God's word. God sent him to tell Ahab that it would not rain until the people went back to worshiping the true God of Israel. After three years of no rain, God sent Elijah back to Ahab. God wanted to

102

show that he was the true God and that he could let it rain again.

Elijah told Ahab, "You are disturbing Israel by disobeying God and following Baal! Come with me to Mount Carmel. Bring the prophets of Baal and all the people."

When everyone came, Elijah said to the people, "You have to choose. If the Lord is the true God, serve him. If Baal is the true god, then serve him." The people didn't know what to say.

Elijah gave them a challenge. "I am the only prophet of the Lord,

and there are 450 prophets of Baal. Let them offer a bull as a sacrifice to Baal. They will put it on the wood, but not light the fire. I'll offer another bull as a sacrifice to the Lord, putting it on the wood without lighting a fire. Baal's prophets can call on Baal, and I will call on the Lord. The God who sends down fire is the true God."

All the people agreed to the challenge.

The prophets of Baal went first. They put the bull on the wood and called out all morning long, "Answer us, Baal!" But nothing happened.

Elijah smiled and said, "Try shouting louder, because Baal might be praying. Or maybe he's taking a walk, or sleeping." The prophets kept calling out to Baal until evening, but still nothing happened.

Then it was Elijah's turn. He took twelve stones, one for each tribe of Israel, and built an altar

to the Lord. Elijah dug a trench around the altar, and then put on the wood, with the bull on top. Next, he poured water all over the wood and the bull. He poured water three times, until everything was soaking wet and the trench was full of water.

Then Elijah prayed, "Lord, God of Abraham, Isaac, and Jacob, let everyone know that you are God and that I am your prophet, following your commands. Bring these people back to their senses!"

At once, fire came down and burned up the sacrifice! It burned up the bull, the wood, the stones, and the dust! It even burned up the water in the trench!

When the people saw all this, they cried out, "The Lord is the true God! The Lord is the true God!"

Then God sent rain to water the earth.

The Prophet Isaiah

Isaiah

Another prophet who spoke God's word to the people was Isaiah. God showed himself to Isaiah seated on a throne with angels all around him. God asked, "Who can I send on an important mission?"

Isaiah answered, "You can send me!"

God sent Isaiah to King Ahaz to tell him to trust in the Lord instead of powerful armies. Isaiah told Ahaz that God wanted him to ask for a sign that would show that God was with Jerusalem and would keep them safe. But Ahaz wouldn't listen.

Finally, Isaiah said to Ahaz, "God himself will give you a sign. A young woman will have a baby boy and

name him Emmanuel."
(This name means "God is
with us.")

"One day there will be a
king from the family of David,"
Isaiah told God's people. "He
will bring peace to the world.
He will be a bright light in the
darkness. He will be joy in sadness. He will help all people to
know the Lord."

When we read these words in
the Book of Isaiah, they remind
us of Jesus, our Prince of Peace.
Other parts of the Book of
Isaiah talk about a suffering
servant who was treated
badly by people. This servant
of God did not do anything
wrong himself, but he took the
punishment for our sins. He
didn't complain when he was
hurt, and his suffering brought
us healing and forgiveness.
These words also make us think
of Jesus, who never did any
wrong, and who died on the
cross to take away our sins.

Jonah and the Big Fish

Jonah 1–4

This story was told long ago to help the Jewish people understand that God loves *everyone,* not just the chosen people of Israel, the Jewish people.

The Lord told Jonah, "Go to the great city of Nineveh and tell the people there that I see all their sins."

But Jonah didn't want to do it. Instead, he got on a ship that was heading the other way. God made a storm come up at sea. The frightened sailors threw whatever they didn't need overboard, to make the ship lighter.

And where was Jonah? He was below deck, sound asleep! The captain woke him up, shouting, "Wake up! Pray to your God to save us!"

The sailors asked Jonah, "What are you up to? Where are you from?"

Jonah answered, "I worship the Lord who made the sea and the land. But I am running away from him."

When they heard this, the sailors were very much afraid. "How could you do such a thing!" they exclaimed.

The storm was getting worse and worse, so Jonah said, "If you want it to stop, throw me overboard." The sailors didn't want to do that. They tried to row even harder. But it was no use. So, they did what Jonah said and threw him into the water. At once, the storm stopped and the sea became calm. The sailors saw this and believed in the Lord.

Then God sent a huge fish to swallow Jonah. While he was in the fish's belly, Jonah prayed to God. After three days, the Lord made the fish spit Jonah out on the shore.

"Now go to Nineveh," the Lord told Jonah. "And deliver my message." This time, Jonah did as God asked.

It took three whole days to walk through Nineveh. Jonah went through the city the first day, crying out, "In forty days Nineveh will be destroyed!" The people realized that they had disobeyed God and they were very sorry. They put on rough cloth and stopped eating to show that they wanted to be forgiven. Even the king of Nineveh put on rough cloth. He ordered everyone in the city, people and animals alike, not to eat or drink, but to call out to God. He commanded everyone to stop doing evil. All the people obeyed the command.

When God saw all this, he had mercy and didn't destroy the city.

Jonah was angry because he wanted God to punish the city. He said to God, "This is why I ran away in the first place! I knew all along that you wouldn't punish these people! You are kind and loving, and don't like to be angry with sinners. Take my life. It would be better for me not to live."

God answered Jonah, "You have no reason to be angry."

Jonah went outside the city and built a hut. There he sat,

watching the city to see what would happen. God made a plant grow beside Jonah to shade him from the sun. This made Jonah happy. But the next morning, God let a worm eat the plant so that it died. Jonah sat in the hot sun. He was very sad and very angry.

Then God spoke to Jonah, "You are concerned about a plant that lived one day and died the next. Shouldn't I be even more concerned about the thousands of my children who live in this great city?" This is how God helped Jonah understand his love and concern for the people of Nineveh.

Judas Maccabeus

1 Maccabees

A time came when the Jewish people were ruled by Greek kings from Syria. These rulers wanted the Jewish people to give up their faith in God. One of the kings went to the Temple in Jerusalem and took the altar, the seven-branched candlestick, and all the things used to worship the Lord. He sent armies to fight against Jerusalem. He told the Jewish people that they couldn't worship in the Temple, keep the Law, or rest on the Sabbath Day. This king wanted the Jewish people to worship the false Greek gods instead.

Many Jewish people would not give up their faith in God. A good Jew named Mattathias, along with his five sons, left Jerusalem and went to live in the mountains. There they worshiped God and kept his Law. Other faithful Jews joined them, and when the king's army came to attack them, they fought back.

115

When Mattathias died, his son Judas Maccabeus took his place. (The name Maccabeus means "hammer.") Judas Maccabeus led the faithful Jews in the fight to be able to worship God in the Temple once more. They remembered how God had helped the Israelites escape from Egypt through the Red Sea. They knew God would help them too.

After winning battles against the Greek armies, Judas led the Jewish army to Jerusalem to take back the Temple. They were sad to see it overgrown

with weeds, but they worked together to fix it up. They brought back everything that had been taken away and had a celebration. They burned incense on the altar and lit the seven-branched candlestick.

Even though there would be more battles, this was a happy time for Judas Maccabeus and his followers. Once more, they could worship God in the Temple!

Every year in December, Jewish people all over the world remember this event during Hanukkah. It is a joyous celebration of the rededication of the Temple, and a time to thank God that they are free to worship him and follow his Law.

New Testament

Mary and the Angel

Luke 1:26–38

God sent the angel Gabriel to a little town called Nazareth, where a girl named Mary lived. Mary was promised in marriage to a good man named Joseph, who was a relative of King David.

The angel said to Mary, "Rejoice! The Lord is with you! He blesses you above all other women!"

Mary was surprised to see the angel! She wondered what his message meant.

Gabriel explained, "Don't be afraid, Mary. God is very pleased with you. You will have a son and name him Jesus. He will be called the Son of God and will be the ruler of Israel forever."

Mary asked the angel, "How can I have a child? I am not married."

Gabriel answered, "The Holy Spirit will make this happen, and your son will really be the Son of God. Even your cousin Elizabeth, who is very old, will have a baby soon. Nothing is impossible for God!"

Mary bowed her head. "I am the Lord's handmaid," she told the angel. "Let everything happen as you said."

Then Gabriel left her.

God's people needed someone to teach them about God. They needed someone to show them how to live. And they needed someone who could take away their sins. This is what Jesus, God's own Son, came to do. He is the Savior God promised long ago to send.

121

Mary Visits Elizabeth

Luke 1:39–56

As soon as Mary learned that Elizabeth was going to have a baby, she decided to visit her. It was a long journey. When Mary arrived, she went to the house where Elizabeth and her husband Zechariah lived.

As Mary said hello to Elizabeth, the baby that was growing inside Elizabeth jumped! Elizabeth felt it. The Holy Spirit filled Elizabeth and she told Mary, "You are blessed among all women, and the child growing inside you is blessed too! How did I deserve to have a visit from the mother of my Lord? You are blessed because you believed that what God told you would really happen!"

Then Mary praised God, saying, "How great God is! Even though I am just his humble servant, he thinks of me. Now all people to come will know that God has blessed me! He is powerful and full of mercy. He remembers his people Israel and keeps the promise he made long ago to Abraham and all his children!"

Mary stayed for three months to help her cousin Elizabeth. Then she went back home.

The words of the angel Gabriel and of Elizabeth have been put together to form the Hail Mary prayer. We can say this beautiful prayer to the Mother of Jesus. When we pray the Hail Mary, we call Mary blessed, because God has done great things for her. Mary praises God for us and asks him to give us all the help we need.

Hail, Mary, full of grace! The Lord is with you! Blessed are you among women, and blessed is the fruit of your womb, Jesus. Holy Mary, Mother of God, pray for us sinners, now and at the hour of our death. Amen.

Jesus Is Born

Luke 2:1–20; Matthew 2:1–11

Before Jesus was born, the Roman Emperor gave an order for all the Jewish people to be counted. To do this, everyone had to go to the town where his family was from. Since Joseph belonged to the family of David, he and

Mary had to travel to Bethlehem, the City of David.

The inns were too crowded, so Mary and Joseph found shelter in a stable where animals lived. While they were there, it was time for Mary's baby to be born. She had a little boy, and wrapped him in swaddling clothes (long, soft pieces of cloth used for babies in those days). Mary and Joseph named the child Jesus, which means "God saves." For a crib, Mary let Baby Jesus sleep in the manger that held the hay for the animals to eat.

Nearby, shepherds were taking turns watching their flocks during the night. Suddenly, an angel from God appeared to them, and a great light shone around them. The shepherds were frightened! But the angel said to them, "Don't be afraid! I have joyful news to tell you! To you is born this day in the city of David a Savior, who is Christ the Lord.

And this will be a sign for you: you will find a baby wrapped in swaddling clothes and lying in a manger."

All at once, the sky was filled with angels. They were all praising God and saying, "Glory to God in the highest and on earth peace to those on whom his favor rests." Then all the angels went back to heaven.

The shepherds hurried to Bethlehem to see for themselves everything that the angel had told them. There they found Mary and Joseph, and Baby Jesus sleeping in the manger. When they told about the angels, everyone who heard it was amazed. Mary kept all these things in her heart and remembered them.

Three wise men in the east saw a special star and followed it to Jerusalem. They asked, "Where is the new-born king? We have followed his star and want to give him honor." The wise men followed the star until it stopped in Bethlehem, right over the place where Jesus was. The wise men bowed down to honor Jesus, and offered him special gifts of gold, frankincense, and myrrh.

Then they returned to their country.

Jesus Is Brought to the Temple

Luke 2:22–40

After Jesus was born, Mary and Joseph brought him to the Temple in Jerusalem. While they were there, a man named Simeon came up to them. He was a holy Jewish man, filled with the Holy Spirit. God told him that he would see the promised Savior before he died.

Simeon took the infant Jesus in his arms. He blessed God, saying,

"Master, now you can let me die in peace. You have kept your promise to me. I have seen the Savior, who will be a light for all people and the glory of Israel."

There was also an old woman named Anna who spent her days praying at the Temple. She came along at the same time and gave thanks to God. Then she went and told everyone about the child who would save the people.

Mary and Joseph brought Jesus back to their own town of Nazareth. He grew up strong and wise, and God's grace was with him.

We call Jesus, Mary, and Joseph the Holy Family. In obeying our parents and getting along with our brothers and sisters, we try to live as the Holy Family lived, loving and helping one another.

Jesus Is Found in the Temple

Luke 2:41–52

Every year, Jewish people traveled to Jerusalem to celebrate the feast of Passover. The year Jesus was twelve, he went to Jerusalem with Mary and Joseph.

On the way home, Joseph traveled with the other men, and Mary traveled with the women. Each thought that Jesus was with the other. But Jesus had really stayed behind in Jerusalem. Soon, Mary and Joseph realized that Jesus was lost! They hurried back to Jerusalem to find him.

After three days of searching, Mary and Joseph went to the Temple. Imagine how surprised they were to find Jesus sitting with all the Jewish teachers, listening to them and asking questions! The teachers were amazed at how intelligent this boy was!

Mary said to her son, "Why did you do this to us? You had us so worried!"

Jesus answered, "Why were you looking for me? Didn't you know that I'd be right here, in my Father's house?"

Then Jesus went home with Mary and Joseph and obeyed them. His mother Mary kept all these things in her heart. She thought about them often. As Jesus grew up, everyone could see he was wise and full of the grace of God.

Jesus Is Baptized

Matthew 3:1–17

Years later, when Jesus was grown up, John the Baptizer began preaching in the desert. John was the cousin of Jesus and Elizabeth's son. "Change your lives!" he cried out. "The Kingdom of heaven is near!"

John was dressed in camel's hair, with a leather belt around his waist. He stayed in the desert, eating grasshoppers and honey. Many people came to hear him preach. Then they would be sorry for their sins and let him baptize them in the Jordan River.

He would say, "I am baptizing you in water so you can change your way of life. There is someone else coming who is greater than I am. He will baptize with the Holy Spirit!" John was talking about Jesus.

One day, Jesus came to the Jordan to be baptized by John. John knew that Jesus was the one to come who was greater than he was. John didn't want to baptize Jesus because he knew that Jesus had no sins and did not need to change his life. But just as Jesus became man to be like the people he had come to save, now he wanted to be baptized along with the others. Jesus loved sinners and wanted to bring them back to his Father.

So, John baptized Jesus. When Jesus came up out of the river, the sky opened and the Holy Spirit in the form of a dove came down on him. Then a voice from heaven was heard. It said: "This is my dear Son. I am very pleased with him."

Jesus in the Desert

Matthew 4:1–11

After Jesus was baptized, he went into the desert to pray for forty days. He did not eat, and he drank only water. In this way, he was getting ready to do the work God gave him to do. By the end of the forty days, he was very hungry. Then the devil came to tempt Jesus, trying to make him think only of himself and not of God.

Knowing how hungry Jesus was, the devil pointed to some stones and said, "If you are God's Son, make these stones turn into bread."

Jesus answered, "People do not live only on bread. Living by the word of God is even more important."

Then the devil took Jesus to Jerusalem, to the top of the Temple. "If you are God's Son, jump down from here. The Bible says that God will send his angels to take care of you so you won't get hurt."

Jesus answered, "The Bible also says that we shouldn't give tests to God to make him prove he loves us."

Next the devil took Jesus to the top of a high mountain and showed him all the kingdoms of the whole world. He promised, "I will give you all these kingdoms if you bow down and worship me."

But Jesus said, "Go away, Satan! The Bible says that we should worship only God!"

Then the devil left Jesus, and angels came to take care of him.

Jesus Calls His Followers

Luke 5:1–16, 27–32; 6:12–16

Jesus began preaching the good news about the kingdom of heaven. One day he was speaking on the shore of a lake. There were so many people trying to get close to Jesus that they were pushing him. Nearby, some fishermen were washing their nets in the water. One of them, named Simon, let Jesus get into his fishing boat. Simon rowed out a little bit from the shore, so that Jesus could teach the people from the boat.

When Jesus finished teaching, he said to Simon, "Go out to deeper water and let down your nets for a catch."

Simon said, "Teacher, my men and I worked hard all night long and we didn't catch any fish. But if you say so, I'll lower the net again."

So Simon, his partners James and John, and the others went out to deeper water and lowered their nets. When they pulled them up again, there were so many fish that the nets almost broke!

Simon knelt down before Jesus. "You should leave me," he said, "because I am a sinner."

137

But Jesus smiled at him and replied, "Don't be afraid. From now on you will be catching people instead of fish." Simon, James, and John brought their boats to the shore. Then they left everything behind and became followers of Jesus.

Another day, Jesus saw a tax collector named Levi (also called Matthew) sitting at his post. "Follow me," Jesus said. Levi stood up, left his tax-collecting job, and became a follower of Jesus.

Soon after, Levi gave a party for Jesus at his house. A lot of the guests were tax collectors and other people who did not follow the Jewish law. When the religious leaders saw this, they told Jesus he should not be making friends with sinners. Jesus explained, "Healthy people do not need a doctor, sick people do. I am calling sinners to change their life. People who think they are not sinners think they have nothing to change."

A while later, Jesus went up a mountain and spent the night praying to God the Father. In the morning, he called all the people who had been following him and listening to his teaching. He picked twelve of them to be his apostles. These twelve men would learn from Jesus by staying with him day and night. They would travel with him from town to town. Jesus would explain his teachings to them apart from the crowd. And when they were ready, Jesus would send the apostles out, giving them power to preach the kingdom of heaven and heal the sick as they had seen him do.

The twelve apostles were Simon, whom Jesus called Peter, his brother Andrew, James and John, Philip, Bartholomew, Matthew, Thomas, James the son of Alphaeus, Simon the Zealot, Jude, and Judas Iscariot, who ended up betraying Jesus.

139

The Wedding at Cana

John 2:1–12

There was a wedding at Cana in Galilee, and Mary, Jesus, and his followers were invited. During the party, they ran out of wine. Mary noticed this, so she told Jesus, "They don't have any more wine."

Jesus asked his mother, "What does that have to do with me? It's not my time yet."

Mary turned to the waiters and said, "Do whatever he says."

Nearby were six very large stone water jars. Jesus told the waiters to fill the jars with water, so they did. "Now take a cup of it to the head waiter," Jesus told them.

When the waiters filled a cup from one of the jars, they were very surprised to see that the water had been changed to wine! They brought the cup to the headwaiter. When he tasted it, he called the groom over. "Usually at a party, you serve the best wine first," the headwaiter said to the groom. "Then after that is gone, you serve the wine that is not as good. But you saved the best wine for last!"

This was the first miracle that Jesus performed in public. He showed the power of God, and his followers believed in him.

Mary had faith in her son Jesus. She knew that he could help the bride and groom when the wine ran out at their wedding party. Even though Jesus had said it was not his time yet, he performed this first miracle when Mary asked him to.

The Woman at the Well

John 4:1–42

One day, Jesus passed through Samaria and stopped near the town of Shechem. His followers went to buy some food. It was about noon, and Jesus was tired from traveling, so he sat down at the town well. A woman came to the well to get water, and Jesus asked her for a drink.

The woman was surprised. "You are Jewish and I am a Samaritan," she said. "How can you ask me for a drink?" (She said this because Jews and Samaritans did not talk to each other.)

Jesus said to her, "If only you understood God's gift, and knew who was asking you for a drink, you would have asked him for a drink, and he would have given you living water."

"But sir," she answered, "you don't even have a bucket! How are you going to get flowing water?"

Jesus explained, "Whoever drinks the water from this well will get thirsty again. But whoever drinks the water that I give will never be thirsty again. The water I give will become a fountain inside the person, flowing up to give eternal life."

The woman replied, "Give me this water so I will never be thirsty again. Then I won't have to keep coming back to this well."

Jesus told her, "Go get your husband and bring him here."

"I don't have a husband," the woman said.

"That's right," Jesus agreed. "Actually, you have had five

husbands, and you're not married to the man you're with now."

"Lord," said the woman, "I can tell you are a man of God. I know a Savior is coming. When he comes, he will tell us everything."

Jesus said, "The one speaking to you right now is the Savior."

The woman left her water jar with Jesus and went into the town. She called to the people, "Come with me and see a man who told me everything I've done! Do you think he could be the Savior?" Then all the people went to the well to meet Jesus.

In the meantime, Jesus' followers arrived with the food and offered him something to eat. "I have food that you don't know about," Jesus said.

"Did someone bring you something to eat?" they asked.

"No," Jesus smiled. "Doing God's will and finishing his work is my food."

They stayed in Samaria for two days. Jesus taught the people and they believed in him. They realized that Jesus really was the Savior of the world.

The living water that Jesus was talking about is the gift of grace. Grace is God's life in us. The Holy Spirit gives us this gift to make us friends of God and God's own children. Grace helps us to live a life of love, as followers of Jesus.

145

The Sermon on the Mount

Matthew 5–7

Crowds of people followed Jesus to hear him speak. He went up the side of a mountain and sat down. His followers sat around him. Now all the people could see him and hear him. Jesus began to teach them:

"If you are poor in spirit, be happy because the Kingdom of heaven belongs to you! If something is making you sad, be happy because you will find comfort. If you are hungry and thirsty for holiness, you will

146

be filled. If you are kind to others, you will be treated with kindness. If you love God for his own sake, you will see him. If you are a peacemaker, you will be called a child of God. Be happy! If people insult you and hate you because you are my follower, be happy! You will have a great reward in heaven!

"You are a light for the whole world. When people see your goodness, they will praise your Father in heaven.

"Do not be angry. When you have a disagree-ment with someone, make up with the person right away.

"Love the people who are unkind to you. This is how you can prove you are a child of God. God lets the sun shine on the good and the bad. He sends rain to the people who do right and to the people who do wrong. Be like your Father in heaven and love everyone.

"Forgive others when they do something wrong to you. After all, your Father is always ready to forgive you.

"Put God first and try to please him. Trust in God for what you need. He loves you and can take care of you better than anyone else.

"Treat others the way you would want to be treated. This is what God's law is all about."

When Jesus finished speaking, the people were amazed. They had never heard anyone teach as he did!

When we read about Jesus teaching on the mountainside, it reminds us of Moses. Moses received the Ten Commandments from God on the mountain, and he brought them down to the people. Now Jesus was on a mountain helping God's people understand more clearly how God wanted them to live. The people who listened to Jesus knew how important Moses was. Now they had a new Lawgiver, God's own Son.

Jesus also taught the people how to pray. The beautiful prayer that he gave us is called the Our Father.

Our Father who art in Heaven, hallowed be thy name. Thy kingdom come, thy will be done on earth as it is in heaven. Give us this day our daily bread, and forgive us our trespasses, as we forgive those who trespass against us. And lead us not into temptation, but deliver us from evil. Amen.

The Daughter of Jairus

Mark 5:21–43

When Jesus and his followers came back across the lake, there was a crowd of people waiting for them. A man named Jairus pushed his way through the crowd. He was a leader in the synagogue (a place where Jewish people pray). Jairus fell at the feet of Jesus and begged him, "My little girl is very sick. Please come and touch her and give her your blessing so she will get better!" So Jesus went with Jairus. A large crowd followed, pushing to keep close to Jesus.

In the crowd was a woman who had been very sick for a long time. The doctors had tried to help her, but they couldn't. Now she told herself, *If I can get close enough to touch the robe of Jesus, I will get well.*

So she pushed her way over to Jesus and touched the edge of his robe. That same instant, she got better!

Jesus felt the healing power go out from him, and he turned around. "Who touched my robe?" he asked. His followers said, "How can you ask that? Look at all these people pushing against us!" But Jesus kept looking for the woman who had been healed.

The woman finally came and knelt before Jesus. She was shaking. "I touched your robe and my sickness disappeared," she nervously told Jesus. Jesus smiled at her and said, "Daughter, it's your faith that made you well. Go in peace. You are no longer sick."

Just then, some people came to meet them from the synagogue leader's house. "Your daughter just died," they told Jairus. "Don't make Jesus come."

But Jesus said, "Fear does no good. What you need is trust." Then he left the crowd behind

and went to Jairus' house with Peter, James, and John.

In the house, Jairus' family and friends were crying loudly because his little daughter was dead. Jesus told them, "Stop crying! The child is only sleeping." They started to make fun of Jesus, but he told them to go outside. Then he went into the girl's room with her parents and Peter, James, and John.

Jesus took the girl's hand and said, "Little girl, wake up." The girl opened her eyes and got out of bed. Her parents were astonished and so happy! "Don't tell others about what I've done," Jesus told her parents, "and give her something to eat now."

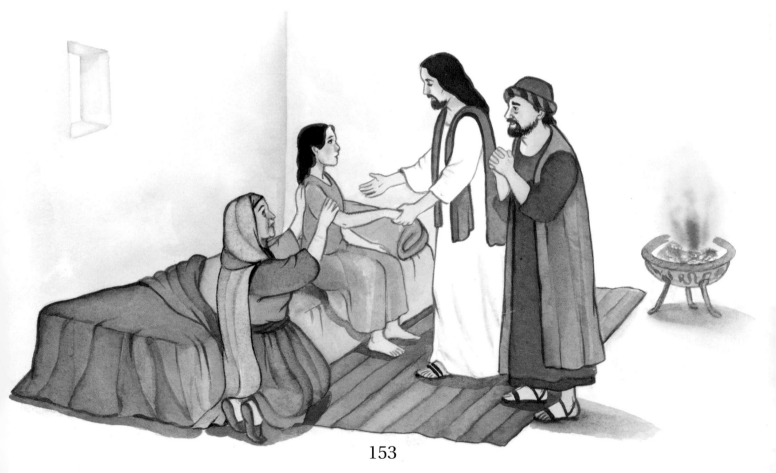

The Miracle of the Loaves and Fish

John 6:1–15

Everywhere Jesus went, a crowd followed. The people wanted to hear Jesus teach and see him heal the sick. One day Jesus and his followers were sitting on a mountainside, and they could see about five thousand people coming towards them!

Jesus knew what he was going to do, but to see what his followers would say, he asked Philip,

"Where can we buy enough bread for all these people?"

Philip answered, "Even if we had two hundred days' pay, we couldn't buy enough bread for each of them to have a bite!"

Andrew said, "This boy here has five barley loaves and two dried fish. But what good would that do for this crowd?"

Jesus said, "Tell everyone to sit down." Then he took the boy's bread and fish and gave thanks. Next, he began to pass the food out to the people. All the people had as much to eat as they wanted.

When everyone was finished, Jesus told his followers to collect the leftovers, so no food would be wasted. They collected twelve baskets of leftovers! When the people saw this miracle, they thought Jesus was like Moses, who had fed the Israelites manna in the desert. They wanted to crown Jesus king, but he left them and went by himself back to the mountain.

Jesus Walks on the Water

Matthew 14:22–33

Jesus told his followers to get in the boat and go across the lake ahead of him. After they left, he stayed by himself on the mountain to pray.

As the twelve apostles were crossing the lake, strong winds began to blow and the water got rough. It was dark now, and it was getting harder and harder to row against the waves.

At about three o'clock in the morning, Jesus came toward them, walking on the water. When his followers saw him, they were very frightened. They started to scream! They thought they were seeing a ghost!

"Calm down!" Jesus said to them. "Don't be afraid! It is I!"

Peter called to him, "Teacher, if it is really you, let me walk to you on the water!"

"Come, then!" Jesus called back.

So Peter climbed over the side of the boat and started walking across the water toward Jesus! But the wind was still blowing as strong as before, and Peter stopped looking at Jesus and started paying attention to the roaring wind. He became frightened and started to sink. "Teacher! Save me!" he screamed.

Jesus caught him and pulled him up. "You have such little faith!" he said to Peter. "Why did you hesitate?"

Jesus and Peter got into the boat, and right away the wind stopped. The other apostles bowed before Jesus, saying, "We know for sure that you are the Son of God!"

Jesus Promises the Bread of Life

John 6:25–69

The crowd that Jesus had fed with the five loaves and two fish crossed the lake to look for Jesus. When they found him, they asked, "When did you get here, Teacher?"

Jesus told them, "You came looking for me because I fed you. Don't work for food that fills you up for a day. Look for the food that will

158

last forever. My Father gives the real manna from heaven, which gives life to the world."

"We want you to give us this food all the time!" they begged him.

Jesus explained, "It is I who am the Bread of Life. Whoever comes to me will never be hungry again. Whoever believes in me will never be thirsty again. I won't turn anyone away, because the Father doesn't want me to lose anyone that he has given me. Instead, he wants me to raise them to eternal life on the last day.

"Moses and the Israelites ate manna in the desert, but they died. Whoever eats the Bread from heaven will never die. I am the living Bread from heaven. The Bread I give is my own body so the world may live."

The people started to say to one another, "How can he give his body to be eaten?"

Jesus said, "You can be sure of this: if you eat my body and drink my blood, you will have everlasting life. My body is really food. My blood is really drink."

Many of the people could not believe this. They didn't think Jesus really meant what he said. But he did. "I know there are some of you who do not believe," Jesus said. "But I speak words of spirit and life."

Because of this, many people who had been following Jesus

left him and would not listen to his teachings anymore. As they walked away, Jesus turned to his twelve apostles and asked, "Are you going to leave too?"

Peter spoke for the whole group: "Lord, whom else would we follow? Your words are everlasting life. We know for sure that you are the holy one of God!"

At Mass, bread and wine are changed into the living Body and Blood of Jesus Christ. We call this gift the Eucharist. Jesus gives himself to us in Holy Communion to be the food of our souls. The words of Jesus in this Gospel story help us to believe in this very special gift that Jesus has given us: the gift of himself.

Peter the Rock

Matthew 16:13–20

One day, Jesus asked his followers, "Who do people think I am?"

"Some say you are John the Baptist," answered one.

"Some say Elijah the prophet," another added.

"Others are telling people that you are one of the prophets, like Jeremiah," said another follower.

"What about you?" Jesus asked the group. "Who do you say that I am?"

Peter spoke up right away, "You are the Savior! You are the Son of God!"

Jesus said to Peter, "How blessed you are! You didn't come to know this from listening to the people. My Father has told you this! And I tell you this: you are the 'Rock,' and I will build my church on this rock. I am going to give you the keys of the kingdom of heaven."

Jesus knew that the time would come when he would be put to death. He knew he would rise from the dead and return to his Father. He was preparing his followers to lead his Church when he would no longer be among them. Peter would have a special position as the leader of the apostles. When Jesus said he would give Peter the keys of the kingdom of heaven, he meant that he was going to put Peter in charge when he, Jesus, returned to the Father.

Jesus Shows His Glory

Luke 9:23–36

One day when Jesus was teaching, he told the people, "If you want to be one of my followers, you must not live for yourself. You must follow in my footsteps, carrying your cross."

About a week later, Jesus went with Peter, James, and John up to the top of a high mountain. Jesus began to pray. But before long, his three followers fell sound asleep. As Jesus prayed, his face and clothing started to shine with a bright light.

All of a sudden, there were two other men on the mountain with Jesus. They were shining with the light of glory too. When Jesus' followers woke up and saw this, they realized that the two other men were Moses and Elijah. Moses delivered God's law to his people, and Elijah was the great prophet of the Lord. Now they were speaking with Jesus about what would happen to him in Jerusalem.

Then Peter spoke up, without really knowing what he was saying. "Teacher," he said to Jesus, "it's so good to be here! We can set up three tents, one for you, one for Moses, and one for Elijah."

Just as he said this, a cloud came over them. It surrounded Jesus, Moses, and Elijah. Peter, James, and John were afraid. Then they heard a voice from the cloud say, "This is my chosen Son. Listen to him."

After the voice finished speaking, Moses and Elijah and the cloud were gone. Jesus stood there by himself.

Peter, James, and John didn't talk about what they had seen to anyone.

On that mountain, God showed Peter, James, and John that Jesus was his own Son. He told them to listen to him and follow his teaching. The cloud that surrounded Jesus, Moses, and Elijah reminds us of God's presence in the cloud that led the Israelites out of Egypt.

The Good Samaritan

Luke 10:25–37

Once while Jesus was teaching, an expert in Jewish law stood up to ask him a question. "Teacher, what do I have to do to go to heaven?"

Jesus answered, "You know God's law. What does it say?"

The lawyer said, "The law says we must love God with our whole heart, soul, strength, and mind. We must love our neighbor as ourselves."

"That's right," Jesus told him. "Do that and you will have everlasting life."

"But who is my neighbor?" the lawyer asked.

Jesus answered him by telling a story. "A man was traveling the road from Jerusalem to Jericho. On the way, robbers stopped him. They took his cloak and money, beat him up, and left him on the side of the road, almost dead.

the man's wounds to help them get better. He lifted the man onto his donkey and brought him to the nearest inn. He got a room and took care of him. The next day, he gave the innkeeper some money and asked him to take care of the injured man. If the innkeeper would need to spend more money to help the

"A priest came walking down the road. He saw the injured man, but went on his way without helping him.

"Next, another man who kept the law of Moses came by. He saw the man but kept going too.

"Finally, a man from Samaria came along. He saw the poor man lying on the roadside and felt sorry for him. He went over, and poured oil and wine into

man, the Samaritan promised to pay him on his way back.

"Which of these three men acted as a neighbor to the man who was attacked by robbers?" Jesus asked.

The lawyer didn't want to say that the Samaritan was the good neighbor. At that time, most Jews had nothing to do with Samaritans. But he had to give Jesus an answer. And so he said, "The neighbor was the person who treated him with kindness."

Jesus nodded and said, "Then that is what you must do, too."

Jesus was showing that we have to be kind to everyone, not just to the people who act the way we would like them to act. Jesus doesn't want us to love only people we think ought to be loved. We are to love everyone without exception because we are followers of Jesus.

The Prodigal Son

Luke 15:11–32

Jesus told another story to show how much God loves us and how ready he is to forgive our sins.

There was a man who had two sons. The younger son went to his father and said, "I want you to give me now whatever money I would inherit from you when you die."

So, the father divided what he owned and gave his younger son the share that was his.

A few days later, the younger son packed his things and took a faraway trip. He quickly wasted all his money on parties and fun. When his money was all gone, there was a food shortage in the land. He had no money and no way of getting anything to eat.

He got a job working for a farmer, who put him in charge of his pigs. The young man was so hungry that even the pigs' food looked good to him, but nobody offered him anything to eat.

Finally, he realized how foolish he was. "My father's servants are well off compared

to the way I'm living. I should
go back to my father and say,
'Father, I have sinned against
God and against you. I don't
deserve to be called your son
anymore. Please just let me
work as one of your servants.'"
The young son made up his
mind to say this to his father
and headed home.

Back at home, his father
was watching the road.
He was thinking of his son
and wondering what had

happened to him. Then, off
in the distance, he saw a
ragged traveler heading his
way. Even though the traveler
was a long way off, and his
clothes were torn and dirty, the
father recognized him. It was
his younger son! His son was
coming home!

The father ran down the road
toward his son. He hugged and
kissed him. The son looked in
his father's kind eyes and said,
"Father, I have sinned against

God and against you. I don't deserve to be called your son…."

But the father was already calling to his servants, "Hurry! Bring him the best clothes! Put a ring on his finger and give him some new shoes! Prepare a feast so we can celebrate! I thought this son of mine was dead, but here he is alive and well! He was lost, but now I have him back!" And they had a big party to welcome back the younger son.

The older son was still working in the fields when all this happened. On his way back to the house, he heard music. "What's going on?" he asked a servant.

The servant said, "It's a party! Your brother has come home and your father has killed the fattened calf to celebrate!" When he heard this, the older son grew angry and wouldn't go inside. His father came out to see what was wrong.

"I've worked for you for years," began the older son.

"I've always obeyed you, but not once did you give me even a kid goat to have a party with my friends. Then this son of yours comes home after wasting all your money and you kill the fattened calf for him!"

"Son," his father told him, "you've been with me all along. Everything I have is yours too. But we have to be happy and celebrate! Your brother was dead, and now he has come back to life. He was lost, and now he is found!"

God our Father is always ready to forgive us, no matter what we may have done. When we are sorry and decide to stop the wrong we were doing, our loving Father always welcomes us back and forgives our sins. God always loves us as his sons and daughters.

Jesus Blesses the Children

Luke 18:15–17

Once when Jesus was teaching, some mothers brought their babies and small children to him. They wanted Jesus to touch and bless their children.

Jesus' followers saw all the children going near Jesus. They didn't think this was right. They thought it was more important for Jesus to talk to the grown-ups and answer their questions. They thought Jesus was too busy teaching to be bothered by the children. So they started telling the children to leave Jesus alone. They told the mothers to take them away.

But Jesus called the children over to him. "Let them come," he said. "Don't send them away." The children gathered around Jesus and he smiled at them, touching their heads and blessing them. "The kingdom of heaven belongs to people who are like these children. If you don't accept the kingdom of God as a child, you won't be able to get into it."

Jesus was giving us an important lesson when he blessed the children. He was teaching us that all of us, even grown-ups, have to become like children in order to be his true followers. We must trust and obey God as little children trust and obey their parents. We must not try to act more important than others do. It's important to love God our Father as completely as a little child loves his or her mother and father!

Jesus Raises Lazarus

John 11:1–54

Jesus had three friends in the town of Bethany. They were Mary, her sister Martha, and their brother Lazarus. One day, the sisters sent a message to Jesus that Lazarus was very sick. Jesus didn't go to see them right away. He told his followers, "The reason for this sickness is to show God's glory."

After two days, Jesus said, "My friend Lazarus has fallen asleep. I will go wake him up." Jesus' followers did not want Jesus to go to Bethany because it was near Jerusalem. The religious leaders in Jerusalem did not like Jesus' teachings. They did not want to believe that he was from God. They wanted to stop him, even to kill him.

"Don't go," Jesus' followers said. "If Lazarus is asleep, that means he's getting better." They didn't know what Jesus meant when he said Lazarus was asleep.

"Lazarus is dead," Jesus then explained. "Let's go."

When they got to Bethany, Lazarus had already been buried in the tomb for four days. There were many friends with Mary and Martha, who were very sad that their brother had died. When Martha heard that Jesus was coming, she went to meet him.

"Lord," she said, "if you had come sooner, Lazarus would still be alive. But even now, God will do whatever you ask."

"Lazarus will rise again," Jesus told her.

"Yes, I know," Martha said. "He will be raised up to life at the end of the world."

Jesus said, "I am the resurrection and the life. Everyone who believes in me will live again, even if he has died. Do you believe this?"

"Yes," Martha answered. "I believe that you are the Savior sent by God." Then she went back to tell Mary that Jesus had come.

Mary ran out to see Jesus. When Jesus saw how sad she was because of her brother, he felt sad too. When Mary brought him to the tomb, Jesus started to cry, because Lazarus had been his good friend.

The tomb was a cave with a big rock closing off the opening. "Take away the stone," Jesus said.

Martha said, "He has been dead four days. If we take away the stone, there will be a terrible smell."

Jesus said, "If you believe in me, you will see God's glory."

They rolled the stone away, and Jesus prayed, "Father, thank you for always hearing me. Let these people know that you sent me." Then he called out in a loud voice, "Lazarus! Come out!"

Lazarus came out, still wrapped in his burial cloths. "Unwrap him so he can move around," Jesus said.

Because of this, many people believed in Jesus. But some people went and told the religious leaders what had happened. The leaders were worried that too many people were following Jesus and listening to him. They were afraid the Romans would destroy the Temple and the Jewish people if Jesus' followers treated him as a king. They decided it would be better to kill one man, Jesus, instead of taking a chance that the Romans would kill all the people. They didn't realize that Jesus really would die to save the whole world.

Jesus Goes to Jerusalem

Matthew 21:1–11

Jesus came into the world to save the world from sin. He would do this by giving his life. Jesus had already told his followers that he would be put to death in Jerusalem, but would rise again on the third day.

Just before the big celebration of Passover, Jesus went to Jerusalem. When they were near the city, he sent two of his followers to a nearby village. "You will find a donkey tied to a post. Bring it back to me," he said. "If someone asks why you are taking it, tell them the teacher needs it."

The two followers went to do as Jesus asked. They found the donkey just as Jesus had said. When the owners asked what the two men were doing, they answered, "The teacher needs it," and the owners let them take it.

When they brought the donkey to Jesus, they laid their cloaks on its back and Jesus got on. A big crowd of people came to meet Jesus. They spread out their cloaks on the ground in front of Jesus as he passed. Some people cut branches from nearby palm trees and laid these down before him too.

Waving palm branches, people shouted, "Hosanna! Blessed is the Son of David who comes in God's name! Hosanna in the highest!"

This is how Jesus went into the city of Jerusalem. The people in the city were asking, "Who is this man?" The joyful people in the crowd waving palm branches answered,

"He is Jesus, the prophet from Galilee!"

Jesus knew that this would be the last week of his life. Every year during Holy Week we remember what Jesus did for us when he suffered, died, and rose to save us from sin.

The most important days of Holy Week are Holy Thursday, when Jesus celebrated the Passover Supper with his followers; Good Friday, when he died on the cross; and Easter Sunday, when he rose from the dead.

The Last Supper

Luke 22:7–38

Jesus sent Peter and John to a certain house in the city where they were to prepare the Passover supper. On Passover, the Jewish people celebrate the time when God led Moses and the Israelites out of Egypt.

In the evening, Jesus and his twelve followers gathered for the meal. He told them, "It's very important that I eat this Passover supper with you before I suffer."

Then, Jesus took bread. He blessed it, broke it, and gave the pieces to each of his followers. "Take this and eat it. This is my body, which will be given up for you. Do this in memory of me," he said. After that, he took the cup of wine. He gave thanks and passed it around to each of them. "Drink from this cup. This is my blood, which will be poured out for you."

Then Jesus told them that one of them, sitting with him

at the table, would hand him over to his enemies. The twelve were surprised to hear this, and asked, "Who could do such a thing?" Jesus knew that it was Judas who would betray him. Judas had already gone to the Jewish leaders and offered to bring them to Jesus. They gave him money, and now he was waiting for the right time.

Then Jesus said to Peter, "I have prayed for you, that your faith will be strong. This way, you will be able to help the others."

Peter said, "Lord, I will stay at your side. I will go to prison and even die with you!"

But Jesus told him, "Peter, before the rooster crows in the morning, you will say three times that you don't even know me."

At the Last Supper, Jesus gave us two wonderful sacraments. In changing the bread and wine to his own Body and Blood, Jesus gave us the sacrament of the Holy Eucharist. When he told his apostles to do the same thing in his memory, he gave them power to change bread and wine into his Body and Blood. This power comes from the sacrament of Holy Orders, by which a man becomes a priest.

Jesus' Last Words

John 14–17

At the Last Supper, Jesus had many things to tell his twelve apostles before he died. In the Gospel of John, we read many of Jesus' last words to them. Here are a few of the things that Jesus wanted his followers to know.

"Don't be afraid or upset. Believe in me. I am going to my Father's house to get a place ready for you. Then you can be with me. I am the Way, and the Truth, and the Life. Everyone who wants to come to the Father, comes to him through me. Whoever sees me, sees the Father, too.

"I am going to my Father. But I have asked my Father to send the Holy Spirit to be with you forever. The Holy Spirit will teach you and help you remember everything I taught you.

"Peace is my goodbye gift to you. Don't be afraid or upset.

"The Father loves me, and I love you. Love each other the way I love you. There is no better love than for a person to give one's life for one's friends. And if you do what I tell you, you are my friends. This is what I am telling you to do: Love one another."

Jesus Is Arrested

Luke 22:39–53

When they finished the Passover supper, Jesus and his followers went to the Mount of Olives, a place where Jesus liked to pray. Jesus said to them, "Pray so that you won't be tempted." Then he went a short distance away from them.

Jesus fell to the ground and prayed, "Father, I would like you to take this cup of suffering away from me. But let whatever you want happen, not what I want." Then an angel came from heaven to give him strength. In his great sorrow, Jesus' sweat became like drops of blood that fell to the ground as he prayed.

When he finished praying, Jesus went back to his followers, but they were all asleep. "How can you sleep?" he asked them. "Wake up! You should be praying that you won't be tempted."

The sleepy apostles blinked their eyes. When they opened them, they saw Judas leading a crowd of people who were against Jesus.

195

Judas went over to Jesus and put his arms around him, kissing his cheek.

"Judas, are you betraying me with a kiss?" Jesus asked sadly.

Next, one of Jesus' apostles took a sword and cut off the ear of the high priest's servant. Jesus said, "That's enough!" Then, he touched the side of the man's head and healed him.

The crowd arrested Jesus and took him away to the high priest. Peter followed, keeping a safe distance behind them because he was afraid. In the high priest's courtyard, some servants were sitting around a fire. Peter joined them. A woman noticed him and said to the others, "This man was with Jesus, too."

Peter was scared. He didn't want to be arrested like Jesus. So he answered, "I don't even know him!"

A little bit later, someone else pointed to Peter and said, "You're one of Jesus' followers!"

Peter exclaimed, "No, I'm not!"

An hour later, someone else said, "He has to be one of Jesus' followers. He is from Galilee."

Once more, Peter denied knowing Jesus. "I have no idea what you're talking about!" he almost shouted. At that very moment, he heard a rooster crowing, and Peter remembered what Jesus had told him: "Before the rooster crows, you will say three times that you don't know me." Then Peter ran away and began to cry. He felt terrible that he had denied knowing Jesus.

Jesus on Trial

Matthew 27:11–34

Early in the morning, the high priest and some of the other Jewish leaders brought Jesus to Pontius Pilate, the Roman governor.

Pilate asked Jesus, "Are you the king of the Jews?"

Jesus answered, "You have said so." After saying this, Jesus did not answer any more questions.

Every year at Passover, it was the custom to release one prisoner. Pilate thought he could get the crowd to let Jesus go. But instead of letting Jesus go free, the crowd chose a horrible prisoner named Barabbas.

"Then what should I do with Jesus?" Pilate asked.

"Nail him to the cross!" they all shouted.

"What has he done wrong?" Pilate asked.

But the crowd only grew louder and fiercer, crying, "Crucify him!"

Pilate was afraid the angry crowd would start trouble if he didn't give in. He washed his hands in a bowl of water to show he wanted to have nothing to do with Jesus' death. But then he told his soldiers to crucify Jesus.

First, Jesus was tied to a post and whipped. Then the Roman soldiers took Jesus' robe off him and put a red cloak around his shoulders. They wove a crown out of thorny branches and pressed it onto his head. Next they put a stick in his hand and pretended to honor him as a king. The soldiers knelt before Jesus, shouting, "Hail to the king of the Jews!" And then they spat in his face.

When they were finished making fun of Jesus, the soldiers put his own clothes back on him, and led him away to crucify him.

199

Jesus Dies on the Cross

Luke 23:23–56

The Roman soldiers led Jesus away. They made him walk through the city to the place where they would crucify him. Because Jesus was so weak, the soldiers made a man named Simon follow Jesus, carrying his cross.

Many people had come out to see Jesus die. In the crowd were some women who were sorry for Jesus and crying for him. Jesus said to them, "Women of Jerusalem, don't cry for me. Cry for yourselves and your children." Jesus was saying that sad times were going to come to Jerusalem.

Jesus was led to a spot called the Skull Place, along with two criminals who were also going to be crucified. The soldiers took Jesus' robe off him and nailed him to the cross, raising him up for everyone to see. They crucified the criminals, one on Jesus' right and one on his left. Then the soldiers rolled some dice to see who would get Jesus' robe.

They also nailed a sign to the cross of Jesus. The sign told why he was being put to death. The sign said, "This is the King of the Jews." People read the sign and made fun of Jesus. "If you are the king of the Jews, then save yourself!" they laughed.

One of the criminals beside Jesus said angrily, "I thought you were supposed to be the Savior! Then why don't you save us?"

But the other criminal said, "Don't you fear God? After all, we deserve our punishment. But this man is innocent." Then he looked at Jesus and said, "Lord, remember me when you are in your kingdom."

Jesus answered him, "I promise that today you will be with me in paradise."

Beginning at noon, the sky darkened for about three hours. In the temple, the curtain in the sanctuary was torn in half. At that moment, Jesus cried aloud, "Father! I give my life into your hands!" Then he died.

A soldier who was watching said, "This must have been an innocent man!"

A member of the Sanhedrin named Joseph asked Pilate if he could take the body of Jesus down from the cross. He wrapped it in nice cloth and buried it in a new tomb carved from rock. The sun was setting and the Sabbath was about to begin. No work could be done on the Sabbath.

Some good women who loved Jesus were watching

from a distance. They decided to come back after the Sabbath. They wanted to bring spices and perfumes for the body of Jesus.

Jesus is really God and really man. Because he is man, he could really suffer and die. Because he is God, his sufferings and death could pay for all the sins of the whole world. This is why we call Jesus our Savior.

Jesus Is Alive Again!

John 20:1–18

Early on Sunday morning, Mary Magdalene went to the tomb. She was one of Jesus' followers. She had watched Jesus die on the cross, and now she wanted to weep near his tomb. But when Mary got there, she saw that the stone was rolled to the side!

She ran to tell Peter and another follower of Jesus. Peter and the other disciple went to see for themselves. When they got to the tomb, Peter went in first and saw the burial cloths, but no Jesus. Then the other disciple went in. As soon as he saw the cloths, he realized that Jesus really was risen.

After they had left, Mary looked inside the tomb. She saw two angels in brightly shining robes. "Why are you crying?" they asked her.

"Someone took my Lord's body away, and I don't know where he is," she sobbed. Then Mary turned and saw Jesus standing in front of her, but she didn't recognize him in his risen body.

"Why are you crying? Who are you looking for?" Jesus asked.

Mary thought Jesus was a gardener, so she said, "Sir, if you took him, tell me where I can find him."

Then Jesus called her by name, "Mary!"

Suddenly she recognized him. "Teacher!" she cried.

Jesus told her, "Go tell the others that I am going back to the Father."

Mary ran to where Jesus' followers were, and told them everything.

We call Jesus' rising from the dead the resurrection. This is proof that Jesus really is the Son of God. Because of the resurrection we know that we can believe everything Jesus taught us. Jesus is our Way to God the Father. He is the Truth, which we must believe. He is the Life, giving his grace to our souls so that we can live as he lived.

Thomas Believes

John 20:19–29

It was Sunday evening. The followers of Jesus had locked the doors of the house where they were staying, because they were afraid. They thought that, like Jesus, they might be killed, since they were his friends.

Suddenly, Jesus was in the room with them. "Peace," he said. He showed them the nail marks in his hands and the spear mark in his side. They were so happy to see Jesus again!

"Peace be with you," Jesus said again. "The Father sent me, and now I am sending you." He breathed on them and said, "Now you have the Holy Spirit. Whenever you forgive someone's sins, they really are forgiven."

Jesus was giving his apostles the power to forgive sins in the sacrament of Reconciliation. In this sacrament, we tell our sins to the priest, and he gives us God's forgiveness.

209

It just so happened that one of the apostles, Thomas, was not with the others when Jesus showed himself to them. The others told him excitedly what had happened. "We have seen Jesus!"

But this was too wonderful for Thomas to believe. He said, "The only way I can believe Jesus is alive again is if I can put my fingers in the nail marks in his hands, and put my hand in the wound in his side."

The following Sunday, Jesus' followers were in the same place. This time, Thomas was there, too. Once again, Jesus stood before them and said, "Peace."

Then he went to Thomas and said, "Put your finger in my hands, and your hand in my side. Don't have any more doubts. Believe!"

Thomas looked in amazement at Jesus. "My Lord! My God!" he exclaimed.

Jesus said, "You believe because you see me, Thomas. How blessed are those who will believe in me even though they do not see me."

We are the people who believe in Jesus without seeing him. We have received this gift of faith in the sacrament of Baptism. Our faith grows stronger when we learn about Jesus and pray to him.

Peter Leads the Church

John 21:1–19

One day, Peter and the other apostles were near the Lake of Galilee. "I'm going fishing," Peter said. The others decided to go, too. They fished all night, but didn't catch any fish.

At sunrise, they saw a man standing on the shore. "Have you caught anything?" the man asked.

"No, nothing," they answered.

"Put your net down on the right side of the boat," the man told them. "You'll catch something."

They did as he said, and their net was so full of fish, they couldn't even pull it up! Then the disciple Jesus loved shouted to Peter, "It's Jesus!" When Peter heard this, he jumped into the water and headed for the shore. The others followed him in the boat. Then Peter went back into the boat and dragged the net full of fish onto the beach.

Jesus had a fire burning on the beach. He was cooking some fish. He also had some bread. They all ate breakfast together.

Then Jesus said to Peter, "Do you love me more than the others?"

Peter answered, "Yes, Lord. You know I do."

Jesus told him, "Feed my lambs." Then he asked again, "Do you love me?"

Once again, Peter answered, "Yes, Lord. You know I love you."

"Take care of my sheep," Jesus said. A third time he asked Peter, "Do you love me?"

Peter exclaimed, "Lord, you know all things. Of course you know I love you!"

"Feed my sheep," Jesus said.

Jesus was getting ready to go back to God the Father. He would soon send his apostles out to teach all the world what they had learned from him. They were the beginning of his Church. Jesus chose Peter to be the leader of the apostles and of the Church. Peter would take care of the Church as a shepherd takes care of his sheep.

We call the leader of the Church the Pope. The Pope stands in for Jesus, who is the Head of the Church. The Pope lives in Rome, but he cares for all the followers of Jesus all over the world. We should pray for the Pope, asking Jesus to keep him safe, and to give him courage and strength for his important job.

Jesus Goes Back to the Father

Acts 1:1–14

For forty days after Jesus rose from the dead, he showed himself many times to his followers, so they could be sure that he really was alive. The last time he appeared to them he told them, "Stay in Jerusalem. In a few days I will send the Holy Spirit to you, just as my Father promised. Then you will

have the courage to tell everyone in the whole world about me."

As soon as he finished speaking, Jesus was lifted up into the sky in a cloud. The apostles kept looking until they couldn't see him anymore.

All of a sudden, two angels were standing with them. "Why are you looking up at the sky?" the angels asked. "Jesus will come back again, in the same way he went up to heaven."

The apostles walked back to the city. They went to the upstairs room where they were staying. There they waited for the Holy Spirit, just as Jesus had told them to do. They spent the time praying together with Mary, Jesus' mother.

217

The Holy Spirit Comes

Acts 2

Jesus' followers waited and prayed with Mary in the upstairs room for ten days. Then, on a special day, something wonderful happened! That special day was Pentecost. Every year on the feast of Pentecost the Jewish people thanked God for the harvest. They also remembered the time when God gave them the Ten Commandments.

Now, on this particular Pentecost, a strong wind blew through the house. Flames of fire appeared above each of the heads of Jesus' followers. They started praising God in other languages. The Holy Spirit had come down on them!

There were many good Jewish people visiting in Jerusalem from different countries. They heard Jesus' followers praising God in their own languages. They knew something wonderful was happening, but they didn't understand what it was.

Then Peter spoke to the crowd. "People of Israel, listen to me! Jesus was sent by God. He worked many miracles to prove it. He was put to death on the cross, but God raised him from the dead. Now we are here to tell about Jesus. He has just poured out his Holy Spirit on us! You must all believe that Jesus is the Lord. He is the Savior sent by God."

Many people believed Peter's words. About three thousand people were baptized that day. This was the beginning of the Church. The believers learned about Jesus from the apostles. They prayed together and celebrated the Eucharist. They lived together, helping one another, and every day more people joined them.

Peter and the other apostles were no longer afraid to be known as followers of Jesus. They preached about Jesus and performed many miracles in his name. Even when the religious leaders tried to stop them, they kept telling everyone about Jesus. The Holy Spirit made them brave.

Saul Becomes Paul

Acts 9

The religious leaders did not like this new Church. They did not want the followers of Jesus to say that Jesus was God. A time came when people were put in jail for believing in Jesus.

A Jewish man named Saul thought the followers of Jesus should be stopped. He got permission to go to the city of Damascus and arrest anyone who believed in Jesus.

As he got closer to Damascus, a bright light flashed around him. He fell down and heard a voice speaking to him. The voice said, "Saul, why are you persecuting me?"

"Who are you?" Saul asked. "I am Jesus," the voice answered, "the one you are persecuting. Go into the city and you will find out what you should do."

When Saul stood up, he was blind! His friends had to lead him into Damascus.

In the city of Damascus was a man named Ananias. Jesus appeared to him and told him to go to the house where Saul was staying. Jesus told Ananias, "I have chosen him to tell the nations about me."

Ananias went and found Saul. He said, "Brother Saul, Jesus sent me to help you see again." Then Saul's eyesight came back. He was baptized and filled with the Holy Spirit.

Saul learned about Jesus from the people in the Church in Damascus. He started to tell others that Jesus was the Son of God.

Saul spent his life traveling to faraway places to tell people about Jesus. He used his Roman name "Paul," because most of the people he preached to were Roman or Greek. Because of Paul, many people who were not even Jewish came to know about Jesus.

Paul gave his life for Jesus. Now he is called Saint Paul. In the Bible, we can read some of the letters he wrote. Saint Paul's letters tell us how we can be faithful followers of Jesus, too.

"I Am Coming Soon"

Revelation 22

At the very end of the Bible, Jesus tells us, "I am coming soon, and I will give each person the reward he or she deserves. I am the beginning and the end, and the bright morning star. I will give living water to anyone who wants it."

Come, Lord Jesus!

227

My Prayers

The Sign of the Cross

In the name of the Father, and of the Son, and of the Holy Spirit. Amen.

Our Father

Our Father, who art in heaven, hallowed be thy name. Thy kingdom come. Thy will be done on earth as it is in heaven. Give us this day our daily bread, and forgive us our trespasses, as we forgive those who trespass against us. And lead us not into temptation; but deliver us from evil. Amen.

Hail Mary

Hail, Mary, full of grace, the Lord is with you. Blessed are you among women and blessed is the fruit of your womb, Jesus. Holy Mary, Mother of God, pray for us sinners, now and at the hour of our death. Amen.

Glory

Glory to the Father, and to the Son, and to the Holy Spirit, as it was in the beginning, is now, and will be for ever. Amen.

The Apostles' Creed

I believe in God,
the Father almighty,
Creator of heaven and earth,
and in Jesus Christ, his only
   Son, our Lord,
who was conceived by the
   Holy Spirit,
born of the Virgin Mary,
suffered under Pontius Pilate,
was crucified, died, and was
   buried;

he descended into hell;
on the third day he rose again
    from the dead;
he ascended into heaven,
and is seated at the right hand
    of God the Father almighty;
from there he will come to
    judge the living and the
    dead.

I believe in the Holy Spirit,
the holy catholic Church,
the communion of saints,
the forgiveness of sins,
the resurrection of the body,
and life everlasting. Amen.

Hail, Holy Queen

Hail, holy Queen, Mother of
Mercy, our life, our sweetness,
and our hope. To you do we
cry, poor banished children of
Eve; to you do we send up our
sighs, mourning and weeping
in this valley of tears. Turn

then, most gracious advocate,
your eyes of mercy toward us,
and after this our exile, show
unto us the blessed fruit of
your womb, Jesus. O clement,
O loving, O sweet Virgin Mary.

Angel of God

Angel of God, my guardian
dear, to whom God's love
entrusts me here, ever this
day be at my side to light and
guard, to rule and guide. Amen.

The Rosary

The rosary is a special prayer
that helps us remember the
lives of Jesus and Mary. While
we think about Jesus and Mary,
we pray the Our Father, the Hail
Mary, and the Glory. We use a
chain of beads called rosary
beads. The mysteries of the
rosary are different events that

we remember in the lives of Jesus and Mary. The chart will show you how to pray the rosary. Before you begin, tell Jesus and Mary about the people you want to pray for. Talk to them about your needs or problems. Thank them for all they do for you.

The Joyful Mysteries

1. The Annunciation—The angel announces to Mary that God has chosen her to be the mother of his Son, and Mary says yes.

2. The Visitation—Mary visits her cousin Elizabeth.

3. The Nativity—Jesus is born.

4. The Presentation—Mary and Joseph present Jesus to the Lord in the Temple

5. The Finding in the Temple—Mary and Joseph find Jesus in the Temple.

The Mysteries of Light

1. Jesus Is Baptized in the Jordan River—John baptizes Jesus.

2. Jesus Works His First Miracle at Cana—Jesus changes water into wine at the wedding feast.

3. Jesus Proclaims the Kingdom of God—Jesus teaches the people about God's kingdom.

4. The Transfiguration—Jesus shines with the light of God's glory.

5. The Institution of the Eucharist—Jesus gives us his Body and Blood under the signs of bread and wine.

The Sorrowful Mysteries

1. The Agony in the Garden—Jesus prays and suffers in the garden.

2. The Scourging at the Pillar—The soldiers whip Jesus.

3. The Crowning with Thorns—The soldiers put a crown of thorns on Jesus' head.

4. The Carrying of the Cross—Jesus carries the cross to Golgotha.

5. The Crucifixion—Jesus is nailed to the cross and dies for our sins.

The Glorious Mysteries

1. The Resurrection—Jesus rises from the dead.

2. The Ascension—Jesus goes up to heaven.

3. The Descent of the Holy Spirit—Jesus sends down his Holy Spirit upon Mary and the apostles.

4. The Assumption—Mary is taken body and soul up to heaven.

5. The Coronation—Jesus crowns Mary Queen of heaven and earth.

1. Make the sign of the cross and pray the **Apostles' Creed.**
2. Pray the **Lord's Prayer.**
3. Pray 3 **Hail Marys.**
4. Pray the **Glory,** name the first Mystery, and pray the **Lord's Prayer.**
5. Pray 10 **Hail Marys.**
6. Pray the **Glory,** name the second Mystery, and pray the **Lord's Prayer.**
7. Repeat steps 5 and 6 until you reach the end.
8. Pray the **Glory** and the **Hail, Holy Queen.**

BOOKS & MEDIA

The Daughters of St. Paul operate book and media centers at the following addresses. Visit, call or write the one nearest you today, or find us at www.pauline.org

CALIFORNIA
3908 Sepulveda Blvd, Culver City, CA 90230   310-397-8676
935 Brewster Avenue, Redwood City, CA 94063   650-369-4230
5945 Balboa Avenue, San Diego, CA 92111   858-565-9181

FLORIDA
145 S.W. 107th Avenue, Miami, FL 33174   305-559-6715

HAWAII
1143 Bishop Street, Honolulu, HI 96813   808-521-2731

ILLINOIS
172 North Michigan Avenue, Chicago, IL 60601   312-346-4228

LOUISIANA
4403 Veterans Memorial Blvd, Metairie, LA 70006   504-887-7631

MASSACHUSETTS
885 Providence Hwy, Dedham, MA 02026   781-326-5385

MISSOURI
9804 Watson Road, St. Louis, MO 63126   314-965-3512

NEW YORK
64 W. 38th Street, New York, NY 10018   212-754-1110

SOUTH CAROLINA
243 King Street, Charleston, SC 29401   843-577-0175

TEXAS
Currently no book center; for parish exhibits or outreach evangelization, contact: 210–488–4123 or SanAntonio@paulinemedia.com

VIRGINIA
1025 King Street, Alexandria, VA 22314   703-549-3806

CANADA
3022 Dufferin Street, Toronto, ON M6B 3T5   416-781-9131